# AMERICA

## A guide
## to the experience

## by David Stuart Ryan

**KOZMIK PRESS** ⊙

134 Elsenham St, London SW18 5NP, UK
PMG, 1506 Capital Avenue, Suite 101, Plano, TX 75074, USA
Astam, 250 Abercrombie St, Sydney, NSW 2008, Australia

Author David Stuart Ryan travelled more than 10,000 miles by road researching this book during three extended tours of the USA. He is a prize-winning poet in America, and has previously written a 'guide to the experience' book about India. He read Ancient History and Philosophy at Kings College, London University.

Editorial consultant: Lisa Norfolk
Production: BPS Book Production Services
Design and Artwork: Nicholas Crossland
Copyright in all photos: David Stuart Ryan, except for those in Chapter 7 which are copyright of Lisa Norfolk

British Library CIP data
Ryan, David Stuart
America: a guide to the experience.
1. United States—Description and travel—1981
I. Title
917.3'04927 E169.02

ISBN 0 905116 16 X (hard cover)    0 905116 17 8 (paperback)

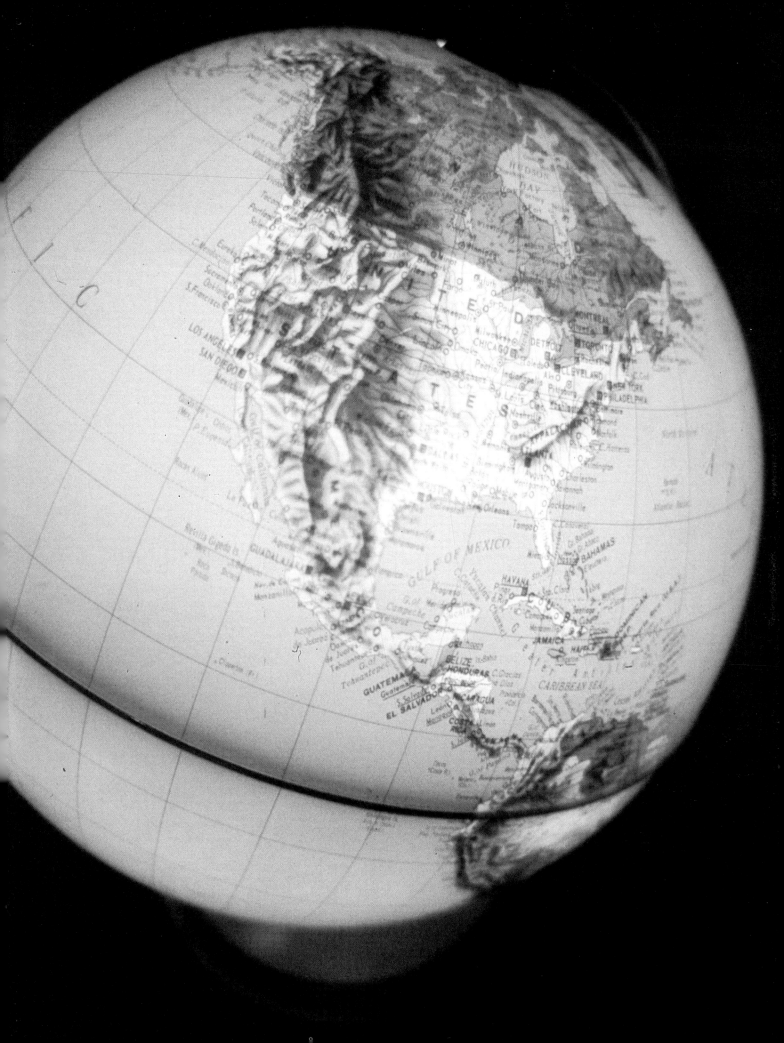

The black man with the grey stubble on his chin, wearing a battered shapeless baseball hat, has drawn up alongside me on the highway into Washington. He is shouting and hollering, seems lost in some arcane insanity that causes him to mouth off his feverish imaginings. I don't respond, carrying on driving, content to listen to the country music coming over the airwaves from a Baltimore radio station. The pilot had said it looked like a 'really warm day' and he was right. The green trees on the edge of the highway into Washington had looked fresh and pretty, it was back to that America of the memory — long roads passing through woody country heading for a destination — with the destination not too important.

But now, as we get nearer town the man in front, who seemed impatient to get a move on, has slowed down. I stay behind him. Finally, at the increasingly frequent red lights I come up alongside him. He again starts bad mouthing me, I raise a hand, palm upwards, shrug, 'What's the big scene man?' He ignores the hand, looks ahead. At least he hadn't pulled a gun. You read about people getting shot for no reason in America. I wonder why he should have zoomed in on me, a visitor just stepped off a plane. Why, at the airport the customs man wanted my autograph when he started reading a book of my poetry as he 'searched' my luggage. That was the public welcoming part of the old Confederacy. You don't find the old New England extremes of cold down here. The black people all around have moved up from further down south and have a drawl that marks them out from faster, more clipped New Yorkers. They have been drawn here by government jobs or the promise of them. The Government has to be an equal opportunites employer if anyone does.

I'm not in too much of a hurry to arrive. Have already stopped at one of those faceless new motel constructions you find on any major road. The father is walking his kids along in his Bermuda shorts, the little boy and girl are cute, entirely unfearful, chattering away, America can't be all that violent a place, you reflect. But if the kids can't feel at home, who can?

It's the run-down outskirts of Washington DC. The Big Mac sign looks welcoming. You know what you're going to get there — wherever you are. It's a measure of the other changes in the environment to sit in that controlled setting. The customers are almost all black. I wonder if I have happened upon a ghetto area. But there sits one white couple in here, a girl and a boy of about 19 or 20 who have only eyes for each other. Again the feeling that it can't be too dangerous a place, even here, if they can blissfully shut out the world and sit, legs intercrossing beneath the table, and talk of their shared mutual happinesss. West Side Story may be a modern myth, but it had its progenitors in people like this couple, the poor whites, you don't see too much of them on the TV screens. The black woman behind the counter says 'Enjoy your meal' in a low key way. You sit down and take it easy, the heat is a midsummer heat near the 80s and the humidity is high. But then Washington is pretty far south.

page 2-3

The Museum of Modern Art, Hollywood Boulevard. It has a large collection of posters, some paintings, some photographs and all those album covers which seemed such landmarks when they first appeared — The Blind Faith cover, Their Satanic Majesties' Request, Sergeant Pepper and more besides. For a 1 am shot, the model looks surprisingly good, that's Hollywood for you.

page 5

The United States are dominated by the Rockies in the West, while the middle of the country is given over to the plains and the mighty Mississippi. The Great Lakes, the Appalachian Mountains, the Tennessee Valley, the Gulf of Mexico all contribute to the diversity of the climate in the East.

Previous page

A shopfront in Washington DC. The 'black is beautiful' slogan of yesteryear has not prevented many black women from wanting to look more Caucasian in their appearance. But there has been progress in the last 15 years. On the West Coast you can find presenters of the main TV news who are seen first as people and only secondarily as black. And that's how they want it to be.

In St Augustine Florida, the oldest town in the USA, you can look at this former market for slaves and get a sense of thousands of wretched Africans being unloaded from the slavers before being sent off to work the fields growing King Cotton. It is calculated that the majority of those captured in Africa died either on the journey or shortly afterwards. The majority of blacks are still be found in the South.

In Washington there are people who come up to ask for a dime in the mean streets just a few blocks away from the White House. There's a man sleeping in a doorway. On 14th Street there are sad and tattered striptease shows with signs saying they have 'the most beautiful girls in town'. But the 'm' in 'most' has fallen off. A white man amongst the predominantly black people milling around in the night, says, 'Here's some reading for you, sir.' You know he's a born-again evangelist. There's the crash of a bottle breaking. You walk on. In the Roy Rogers hamburger bar further along, a sleekly muscled roller skater comes in and chats to a friend who says he's heard of a job going at $50 a day. The informant is well-dressed in a blazer. He skates out the shop, crosses the road, nearly collides with a car that he only just avoids by throwing himself into a tight controlled circle.

In the Dupont Plaza there are impeccably dressed blacks, an extended family, seemingly in their Sunday best, visiting town for Memorial Weekend. They contrast with the casual squalor of the downtown streets where the Government seems resolutely set on not being seen to spend money lavishly on urban renewal. The roads are patchily surfaced — but mercifully have not been allowed to degenerate into great potholes as in the Big A. This street level meanness makes the sudden splashes of wealth seen at the Kennedy Center and the Marriott Hotel, where white coated doormen park the guests' immaculate limousines, seem all the more of a contrast.

There are many levels in America you realise. The poor living right amongst the rich. The Government seems to operate a hands-off policy unlike Europe where the contrasting extremes have been obliterated, at least partially, by taxes and welfare payments and public planning and state aid. You sense the underlying ethos, the public streets are mean streets for some, you have to fight your way up from here into one of those comfortable buildings that can look very desirable indeed if you haven't a dime.

'Hey man, how's ya day?'

'Fine.'

'Can you spare some change for a coffee?'

It's 7-30 in the morning, the streets are almost empty. It's a grey stubbled black man gladhanding me.

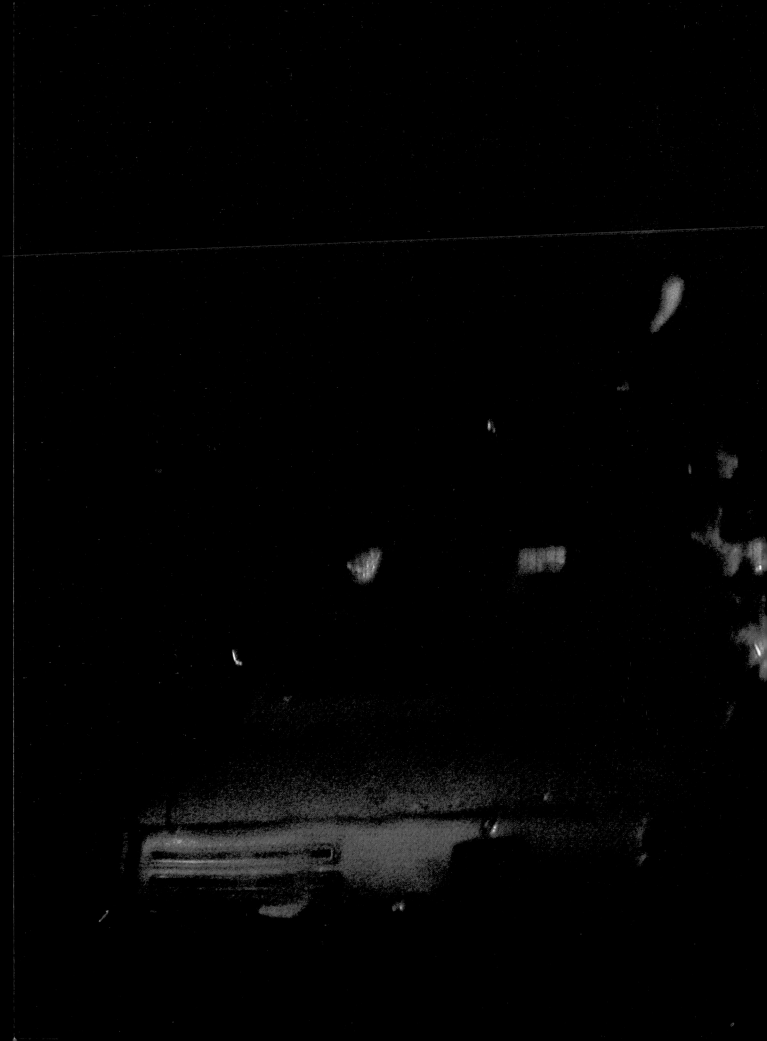

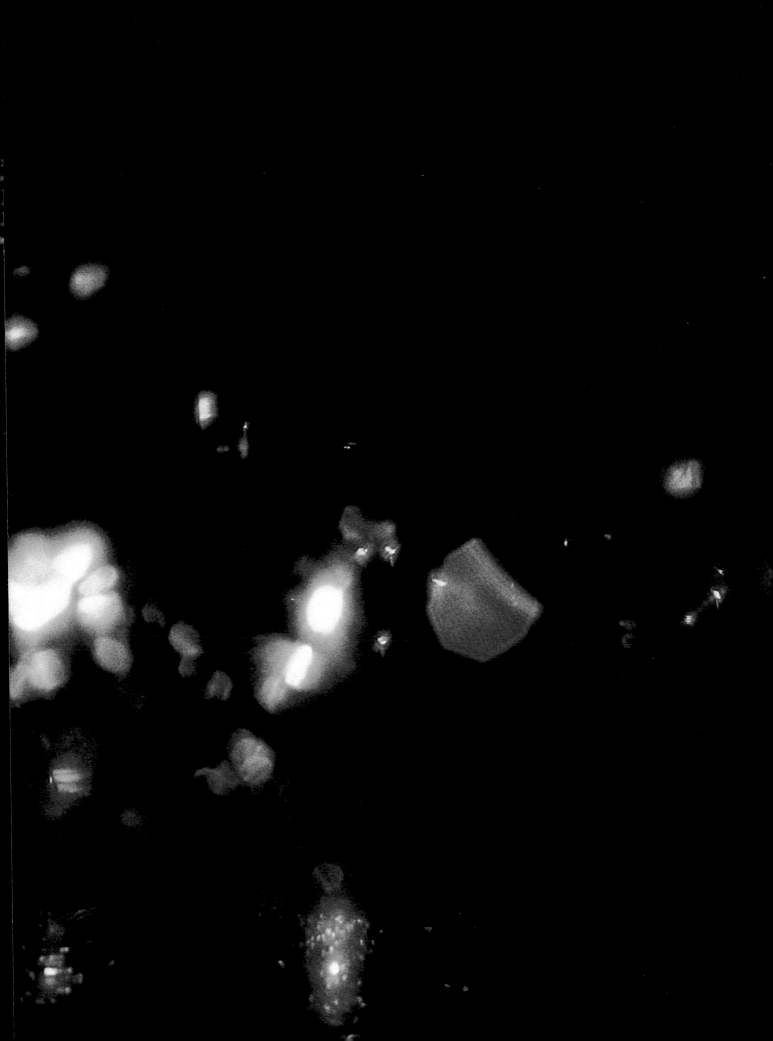

In the palm-tree studded area of the hotel bar, the Mexican barman does not take too kindly to the small Jewish waiter trying to show him how the cash till works. The waiter has all the characteristics of the displaced mid-European Jewry of pre-World War II Europe. Diffident, intense, rather anxious, eager to get on. He may have been in America a long time — but for him the promised El Dorado has not arrived. However, he does attend those for whom the dream of affluence has come true. He is proximate to wealth. Perhaps that is all he desired.

And as you survey those sitting at the bar at 12-30am, you become aware of the heavily weighted odds in favour of native-born Americans of north European ancestry. I am talking to a cartoonist from upstate New York who describes the process of Americanisation that precedes acceptance by a fluid society which, for all that, has its avenues of advancement clearly delineated. The cartoonist's wife is the daughter of Lithuanian immigrants. They settled in a tight little community of fellow Lithuanians. Yet she, having attended school and been born in the country, regards herself as an American with some interest in her origins, but not a great deal. Her husband explains that he has some Irish and English ancestry along with a touch of Mexican. But 'Both my parents were illegitimate — I can only trace half the story'. So the man who knows he is American does not know too much of his antecedents.

'There was a big revival in family genealogy around the time of Roots,' he explains, 'but not so much now.'

So the assimilation of the immigrants goes on. The white Protestants still tend to marry one another. The Catholics too. Though Catholics now make up 23% of the population and form the biggest single church group (ahead of the Baptists with 16%), they are also the newer immigrants' descendants. Those who came from a troubled Europe in the years around the turn of the century and on into the 1920s before the Depression hit and temporarily ended the onward sweep of the economy. They are poorer than the WASP elite. Heavily represented in the blue collar jobs where they offer their labour and their manual skills. But many of the old 'smokestack' labour-intensive industries are in long-term decline. It is the new technologies that are providing the jobs now, those that demand a higher level of education and training. In California, home of the 'sunrise' industries, 1 in 10 of the working population possesses a degree. The premium is on new skills that require years of schooling to acquire.

No wonder that many of the blacks feel dispossessed. The Jesse Jackson candidacy revealed a surge of awareness that the ballot box offered a potentially powerful remedy for the accumulated ills visited upon them. The young, in particular, saw the preacher-turned-politician as a direct inheritor of the Martin Luther King campaign for greater equality. But there is also a sense that it will take another generation for all those high ideals to be turned into some form of reality.

Previous page

Washington DC on a dark wet night near the Watergate complex. The unravelling of the threads that led to the President's office probably could not have been achieved without the assistance of 'Deep Throat', the most likely candidate for this role being Haig. It was reported that the distraught Nixon took to wandering through the White House talking to pictures of past presidents, shortly before he quit.

The Garden Bar of the massive Shoreham Hotel in Georgetown. All rates at American hotels are negotiable so don't take the first price they offer, especially at weekends. If paying by credit card it's now normal for them to check it out when they ask to 'take an impression.'

In the meantime, the lobbies of the top hotels — the Hilton, the Regency Hyatt, the Shoreham — contain a variegated collection of Americans. Their backgrounds hinted at in the name tags the delegates are wearing. But they have a shared lifestyle that places the emphasis on smart, colourful clothing, a gleaming wholesomeness. The immigrants and, often, their children have yet to break into these charmed circles. The Washington suburbs in areas like Georgetown reveal the divide. The mean, downtown streets give way to lovingly groomed gardens profuse with greenery. Signs on the side of the road advertise that this is a community that 'reports all suspicious activity to the police'. The baseball players in the Georgetown park prepare for a match against a black team but there are few blacks who actually live here. The old town has qualities preserved from colonial America, the days of the Confederacy.

In the bars, in the coffee houses, the young sit and debate loudly — removed from the downtown streets that at 3am are still strolled by an almost entirely black population. Bottles crash into pieces in the night, cars drive incessantly by, the city is a long time going to sleep, a restless energy drives the people. A man comes hammering on a door at the downtown bus terminal hotel. The rooms are bare floored, with a perfunctory washbasin. Stark. It is gone three. He is looking for a man.

'I thought you were my friend,' he bitterly complains at the door.

But he's locked out. Dispossessed. His friend won't answer him as he pleads outside the door of his room. It is not easy to come off the mean streets.

There is a breakfast meeting at the American Booksellers Association convention. The speakers are Lee Iacocca — formerly of Ford, now of Chrysler — and Rosalynn Carter — formerly of the White House, now of Plains, Georgia. The meeting takes place at 8am, and every seat is taken. That tells you something about American get-up-and-go. Rosalynn Carter seems very sweet but you suspect she really ran the Presidency. A southern belle with all the old American grit in place. Lee gives the low-down on how they got him out of Ford, free speech is a much-valued American constitutional right which the people endearingly take literally as they tell it like it is. And here is Carole Baron saying that she read every book in the children's library, went on to the adult section and was then caught in the act of taking out a book with a red star. She lost her membership and graduated to the paperback stacks of her hometown drugstore. Today she runs Dell, one of the nation's biggest paperback publishing houses. She can't be more than 40.

There is also a recently retired reviewer from the New York Times on the stand. He, too, expounds on the American way of making information available. He explains how Castaneda's seminal work started off as a doctoral thesis, until a smart publisher saw the potential.

All this earnestness and awareness of where they have come from, the sense of being 'honoured' with an influential position, these are very American characteristics. There is no European *haute grandeur* about the people, rather a realisation that personal effort and the indefinable system have put them where they are today.

And here is Erica Jong signing her books. She certainly doesn't need to do this now, not after that multi-million seller 'Fear of Flying'. Yet she continues to meet her supporters looking older, sadder, wiser ... still an incurable romantic ... weighed down with her knowledge of the fall.

Americans at work and play give it all they've got. Quickly establishing who you are, why you're here, what you expect. Just as succinctly defining themselves. After 20 minutes of conversation the 30-year-old woman from New York starts to talk about a new bestseller.

'It's called 'How to get what you want from a man.' It's all about getting money. Nothing about mind or spirit. The woman's movement hasn't taken us any further forward than 50 years ago.'

And yet even to have defined that it is the quality of the relationship that needs to be improved, denies her observation. If America is the home of militant feminism, it is even more the home of self-awareness. The women are prepared to ask for what they seek and to take part in the experiment of adjusting their values along the way. Not all, or even many, blame men for their problems.

The party is in full swing. Even 10 years ago you would not have seen the women giving themselves up to an abandon like this, as they shake their hips far more uninhibitedly than the men. They are enjoying being females capable of open desire. On the hot dance floor it is like 'a New York party'. You can barely move, let alone dance. All around a great ruck of bodies gyrate and beat time to the music. It doesn't take too much for inhibitions to be shed here. Yet, it is also business. Cards

Previous page

The unknown soldier from Vietnam lies in state under the rotunda of the Capitol Building. This 1984 attempt to finally lay to rest the divisiveness that the war produced in American society has been only partially successful. The reluctance of the government to increase taxes to pay for the war resulted in an inflationary situation as money was simply printed.

collected at the door by the Berkeley Publishing Company. Huge towering bouncers to keep out the curious passers-by. Within the confines of this self-selected gathering, the need to make contacts and possible future deals has overcome the contradictory impulse to remain separate. This is a society that defines people by what they do rather than what they are.

Any conversation quickly leads you back to this reality. 'My boss is being demoted, they've promised me promotion,' the 30-year-old gratuitously says. 'American companies like to move their top executives around. No, they're not firing him, putting him in charge of special projects. It gives him time to look around. I used to be a secretary, I've had four job changes in seven years with the company. Now I'm a product manager.'

Enjoy it while it lasts seems to be the only worthwhile advice. The rise may be spectacular, but there is always the downside, the fall. It comes across in the speeches of those who have come out of the economic machine and relinquished their hold on day-to-day power. They are being paid to publicly ruminate on the experience, for consumption over breakfast.

The swirling currents, that wash up against the rocks of your position in America, can be the ultimate aphrodisiac you realise. Once you're a powerbroker, it seems very boring to be left high above the tideline. The splash of the sea spray is exhilarating indeed, and a little dangerous.

A woman lawyer who processes up to 600 application a day from Hispanics who want to lawfully settle in the USA. She is remarkably candid about how difficult it is to remove even illegal immigrants. They have some rights under the Constitution. In spite of the law-breaking, reverence for the law in America is finally stronger in Europe, thanks to the Supreme Court's independence as granted in the Constitution.

# WASHINGTON ~ A CAPITAL CITY

It was in the 50s and 60s that Washington suddenly grew up. Within the amorphous miles of the District of Columbia, the capital sprouted in all directions. Today, more than 3.2 million Americans live here if you include the sprawling suburbs. Many, if not most of these people, work for the Fed in some way. The Pentagon alone is like a city within a city. But the longer you stay in D.C. the more the underlying inheritance — that of a small town that very nearly joined the Confederates — shows. Everyone seems incredibly polite, a hangover from the genteel days of the plantation owners who ran mini-kingdoms and who could afford to be polite to their acquaintances when their work was done by some 4 million slaves.

It is those former slaves who have flocked to the capital while retaining their southern drawl. That is the true sound of streets. Even though it was intended to be a neutral place where a Californian or a Nebraskan or a Yankee or a Midwesterner would feel at home. The lush suburb of Georgetown retains its old colonial character with neatly tended gardens, modestly sized houses and a lazy lifestyle. Just as in Confederate times, the blacks are hardly in evidence here. They are downtown, clustered near the white gleaming Capitol building and the approaches to it. More than 2/3 of Washington's population is black or brown. Newer minorities are helping to turn the city into a safe haven for the oppressd and poor who used to be welcomed — if that is the word — at Ellis Island.

The Vietnamese and Cambodians have settled around Washington in large numbers. Many are illegal immigrants who intend to stay. Calculations vary between 6 and 12 million for the number of illegal immigrants in the country. They supply the cheap labour for service industries where not too many questions are asked in return for 75 cents an hour. Most of the illegals are from El Salvador and Mexico. They walk across the long border, some come smuggled in trucks, even strapped under car's suspensions. If they escape the 'highwaymen' who lie in wait for them in the border zones, they disappear into the country. These people quickly learn that they can appeal for their rights under the constitution and look forward to a likely eventual acceptance. Even non-residents have some rights in America. I speak to a woman lawyer who processes up to 600 applications from Hispanics in one day — in her mind there is not much that can be done about them, especially if they claim refugee status.

These 'refugees' seem to be the most visible indication of where American money is being spent abroad. The Vietnamese, for example, who sit on the green grass beside the Washington Memorial — all in their late teens it seems — chatter in their native language. A man of about 40 is holding a 9-month-old baby in his arms. He's proud of her, shows her off to passers-by, she is after all an American. A large limousine draws up and two of the Vietnamese on the grass climb in the back. In the front sit probable relatives who have already prospered in their adopted land. The assimilation process in America is a rapid one. And today, the last untidy remains of the war that brought these people here in their hundreds of thousands are being tucked away.

'Equal justice under law' proclaims the stirring legend on the Justice Building in Washington. The Presidential powers of executive action are balanced by the legislative powers of the Congress, and both of these are kept in check by the judiciary. Equal rights for black people remains the largest omission from the country's record on human rights.

Previous page

A musician and friend do their bit for a New York publisher. 'Put on a happy face' is very much part of the American philosophy, as is 'Pick yourself up, dust yourself off and start all over again'. The best of the Hollywood musicals successfully put on the screen the folklore of the optimistic immigrants out to create a new life.

The unknown soldier. One of more than 2,500 still unaccounted for in that long war. The missing, who the Americans forlornly hope to trace, if ever diplomatic relations were established with Vietnam. But that would be difficult. A 'grump' — veteran — described the trauma of being there like this. 'I was talking to my buddy. The next second there was only a foot and piece of knee left.'

'Post-trauma stress' is how the authorities describe the victims' actions, they are often still bearded, scruffy, coming to terms with the society that sent them into the madness. 800,000 are reckoned to be so affected. 100,000 are reputed to have committed suicide. There is always a final reckoning.

In the cleansed Capitol building where the Congressmen fought a long battle to win back control of the war, the unknown solider lies in state. Cameras noisily click. A group of beer-bellied men wearing peaked caps cluster together looking at the coffin draped in the Stars and Stripes flag. Neat as a pin, prematurely grey, his wife and small daughter beside him, a man surveys the coffin from his wheelchair. Two stumps of legs immediately reveal his grief. He sits upright with his arms folded — sharing in a moment of reflected glory before finally fading from the American consciousness and into history. A ragtag collection of 'grumps' joined the tail end of the funeral procession through town but this Memorial Day the town and the nation is laying to rest the ghosts of that war. The generation called upon to fight it, or to resist it, has proved harder to assimilate into the great consensus of American politics than any since the Civil War. In the business of the nation, employers try to jump to the next generation, more obedient, less inclined to question authority, but it is no guarantee against the ground swell in the country led by these dissidents who do not find the complacency of the Reagan years enough.

Now that the divided nation has learnt to let go of its prejudices from the time of polarisation, the items on the agenda from the Nam days have to be debated. Old visions and dreams, old scores to be settled, the now not-so-young against the now infirmly-old. Just when the world and even the country believes it has acquired some sort of stability the rules of the game change again. That too has always been America, nothing stays the same too long.

Reagan, wiping away tears of fancy, commends the unknown soldier into the arms of his maker. Extolling the example of the college kids who had applauded a group of veterans in a Washington cafe. They are neat and tidy these youngsters. The girls uniformly dressed in jeans, and chewing gum. Fast in their movements, restless in their energy, the teenage boys and girls sit chattering in the Roy Rogers fast food restaurant. They were hardly born when 58,000 soldiers went off to die, and the new leaders are fearful of sending them off on a similar reckless adventure. The youngsters know that, and it gives them a remarkable assurance.

Situated in Pennsylvania Avenue, the center of the country's power looks homely enough, A group of actors and actresses pose in front of the railings on a stop-off during a tour of the country. It is a place of pilgrimage for the ordinary American who needs reminders of a united democracy in a land where the rights of the states have still not been clarified completely — the issue which occasioned the Civil War.

'Slow your speed sir, you were doing 73mph in a 50mph area,' the traffic cop informs me. The light flashing in the car mirror, the police car zooming up with its red, white and blue warning light across the roof, produce a sense of disbelief. In the cities and their outskirts, at least, the speed limits are enforced rigorously. Most Americans seem happy enough to saunter along at 55mph in their soft suspension cars. The cars themselves are getting smaller but the dream for many Americans is still the big swanky limo.

The automobile has revolutionised America. There are more cars here than in any other country, and the most abiding image for any driver is of the forest of road signs on the approach to any medium-sized town as retailers fight for your attention and custom. Down the back roads the cars disappear into the rain-dark night. Here is the true country with miles of empty road through unbuilt-upon land. You alone with the DJ playing songs to suit the soaked conditions.

In the morning the Toms River DJ announces that the weatherman is calling for the rain to finally stop by mid-afternoon after a 4-day spell of continuous downpour. Ocean County, New Jersey, plays host to mile after mile of first and second homes along its Atlantic coast. It is quiet semi-suburban America. The school bus driven by a mother stops to pick up two more passengers — its yellow warning lights piercing the gloom. Quietness returns to this township by the sea, where most of the houses have a small boat outside, where canals thread between the small, usually white houses. Now you can hear the birds sing, the sea though cold is unpolluted. America seems all new again.

Yet you are only 100 miles from the hubbub of New York City. As the turnpike nears the grey blocks of the city, the six lanes of traffic increase their pace, huge trucks thunder by, everyone seems to be travelling at 65mph as the Big Apple approaches. The Parkway by the Hudson River is a veritable race track with a driver cutting in front of the cars first on one side of the road and then on the other, propelled by the urge to get into the grid of streets that is the city.

The turnpike — with its frequent dollar and quarter tolls — is made-up well enough. So it is no preparation for the assault upon the car suspension that New York's streets commence. But you are too busy looking out for errant cars at intersections (red lights are only reluctantly obeyed) to worry about potholes.

'Step on the gas man, and then they'll have some respect for you,' a tightly-curled young black urges a truck driver, as he tries to stop the traffic with a mixture of hollering and waving so that the truck can reverse out onto Columbus. New York is an aggressive city, and that is reflected in the way they drive. A taxi screeches to a halt, narrowly missing two pedestrians.

'It said walk,' the pedestrian in a suit complains. The taxi driver just glowers, his passenger looks amused.

The city's traffic attendants suffered over 500 assaults last year. To hit them is only classified as a misdemeanour, unlike the punishment for striking policemen or firemen. The traffic attendants continue to enthusiastically ticket and tow away cars so that even having successfully navigated the roads, it is still problematical to find a parking spot.

Previous page

A wet dawn in Ocean County, New Jersey. Even though little more than 100 miles from New York City, the land has reasserted its hold over the inhabitants. They nestle in groups along the vast coast in their clapboard houses and lapse into that American dream of living in an earthly paradise.

However the increasingly speedy drive into New York City is a good preparation for the assault upon the senses that the city unleashes.

The Dakota Buildings. The doorman confirms, with a wince in his tough face, that this is where John Lennon was shot. The dark entranceway is the frame for a man to emerge from inside the building. He is long haired and going grey, striding with a jaunty step. How John Lennon would have looked if he had still been alive. But then he never expected to live past 40, and he was right.

If you are a stranger in this city they are not going to trust you, no sir, not when credit card fraud gangs have cleaned up over $500,000,000 dollars; one of the two major gangs operates from New York, forging cards from the carbon copies of receipts. At the hotel the receptionist passes the card through the telephone link with the central computer. Back comes the answer. 'Decline.'

The clerk tears up the just-completed slip. 'Do you have any other credit cards?' she asks disdainfully. It takes an urgent and begrudged phone call to the all-knowing HQ of the credit card company to explain that your payments are being recorded almost as you make them, can they extend the limit?

New York without any money looks a very different place. You notice all the people on the sidewalks selling $5 purses, inflatable dolls emblazoned with 'kiss me' for two bucks, Martian headpieces for only a buck. Some people never do get off the streets. Fortunately the cheaper hotels have yet to get wired into the world credit bank where a step over the limit is policed with a new kind of efficiency. Instant retribution has arrived.

The entrance to the Dakota Buildings where John Lennon was shot in 1980. Lennon had chosen to live in New York because it was one of the few places he would walk around without being mobbed. The super-cool New Yorkers would generally do little more than say 'Hi' if they passed him in the street. Mark Chapman was not from New York however.

'New York City is the best city in the world,' says Sarah with a winning smile, half expecting to provoke a negative response which she will determinedly extinguish. She continues. 'There are three bad things about the city. No trees. Dirt. Crime. Apart from that, it has everything. I think after dark New York looks really exciting. I've lived here three years and nothing bad has happened to me. Of course, I was living in the village and that's nearly all gay. I could walk around anytime of night or day and never be hustled but it's not really my scene. I mean it cuts out half the options. Now I'm looking around for an apartment near the low 40s on the Hudson River side. It's the last part that hasn't been developed. If I could afford to buy it would be smart. You know it cost me half my wages, $500 a month, just to rent a small room down in the village. Working freelance, being a woman, meant you never got paid on time. I had a cashflow problem, that's why I moved back home but I think around August I'll start seriously looking. There's lots of ethnic places with young professionals moving in — you know, you find a neon-lit hi-tech restaurant next to a Chinese laundry.'

Sarah is a young professional (25) herself, in advertising. She knows she's lucky to have got in after a lot of persistence, so perhaps her enthusiasm for the place in the sun she has won is understandable. In the village there's a sense of being in an area where people actually live. Dogs being walked. Small neighbourhood grocery stores. The gay men have become very cliquish, the area has unobtrusively been taken over by them. It started in 1969 when they rioted but in this place of more than brotherly love there is a conspicous absence of the aggressiveness that permeates the streets near Central Park — Lennonland. The prices are lower here too. You can expect to pay $750 upwards anywhere near the Park for even the tiniest 'studio'. The city has enjoyed a rebirth in the last 10 years as generous tax allowances have encouraged new building. The developers are expected to give a *quid pro quo*.

An alleged fraud case is in the papers — a small example of the money involved in New York real estate. A medium-sized office block was allowed to be built on the condition that the rents to tenants were 'capped' i.e. set at a reasonable level, at least for the first tenants. At the same time as the City Planning Dept was being told that rents would total approximately $½ million, the mortgage company was being assured that rents would bring in near to $1million a year. In return for the privilege of building in prosperous Manhattan the company agreed to renovate the approaches to a subway station. (The New York subway is not quite the hellhole it's depicted to be, but it's certainly rundown). The developers were unfortunate in their tenants. Claims totalling several million from them brought out the linen to be washed and aired in public. The City demanded back over $7million in allowances. At the 11th hour the developers hired the former lawyer to the City Planning Dept as their representative in the case, since he had just gone into private practice. Result. The successful challenging of the City Dept, the re-examination of what precisely the developers had agreed to. You don't have to be smart (and New Yorkers pride themselves on being one step ahead) to realise how much a former public employee with his knowledge of the bureaucracy is worth in fees, especially as many American lawyers get a share of the award in any successful case.

**Opposite page**

Skyscrapers on Madison Avenue, New York City reflected in another skyscraper's mirror finish exterior. The buildings dwarf the people and are intended so to do.

**Previous page**

A tunnel burrowing under the sea to Maryland from Washington. All over America are huge tunnels and bridges linking up the centers of population in a spectacular demonstration of the country's wealth and engineering abilities. Many of these are the legacy of President Johnson's 'Great Society', a period when the infrastructure of today was laid down.

New York. Head office city. The place where the megabucks are spent. All-hustling city. Sackloads of applicants for jobs on Madison Ave, Fifth Ave, Third Ave, where the gleaming skyscrapers soar up from the chaotic streets. Here is a street vendor whose stock of sunglasses is being seized by a policeman. The street vendor protests as the photographer takes his shot and disappears into the crowd of office workers leaving their havens of industrious activity. It's very mean on the streets. The office workers walk purposefully along. The men in their neat lightweight suits clutching briefcases. The women expensively coiffured. You enter a building. The commissionaire takes down your name and purpose of visit. Up the elevator are new avenues of offices, with a name on each door. They are empty mostly. It's Friday evening. A girl comes in, looking shocked. 'I just heard something terrible.'

'What?'

'Oh, you don't want to hear.'

'No tell us.'

'A friend of mine went to Maryland with a group of people. She got separated from them at the races and asked someone the way to the bus station. The guy told her to follow him down a small alleyway then did just about everything to her. Her face is unrecognisable. Her eyes are completely bloodshot from him trying to strangle her. She's got two broken ribs (all recited in a quiet factual voice). She's pretty, about my age, 28 or 29. And that was Maryland, not New York.'

A pause in the office.

'The only thing you can say is at least she got out of it alive.'

'That's what she said.'

The girl is looking forward to her weekend sailing off the coast. She bids goodbye, smiling, clutching a box containing a new stereo system. That's New Yorkers for you.

Opposite page

The entrance of Time Inc's headquarters at the Rockefeller Center in New York. The large American corporation has an income equivalent to some poorer countries in the world, and in the best of them it has produced a Medici-like consciousness of the duties that come with power. Founder Henry Luce, perhaps because of his Jesuit education, sought to wield influence as much as to make money. Time magazine continues to be middle America's bible on current affairs.

The evening rush hour in New York. Two girls leave work and head for the subway where they are more than likely to begin a journey that will take them to the suburbs that extend up to 50 miles away. Only the very rich and people sharing can afford to live in the central district.

Waking up in New England you might think you had been spirited away back to that land across the ocean — England. Once there was 'new this' and 'new that' all along the coast as the arriving Europeans sought to build 'a shining city upon the hill that would act as a beacon for all men.' It is still in fact the true American dream, this Puritan vision. The landscape is European in its cast, church spires rise from behind clumps of trees, sailing boats are moored in creeks, a languid relaxation is in the air. There's a reproduction Pilgrim village now, and a reproduction Mayflower, actors are employed to go about in 17th century costume speaking in 'English' accents. Confront them with a real English accent and they suddenly 'dry up'.

But however British the New England landscape may appear, the architecture is definitely American. In the small towns there's still an emphasis on clapboard houses with a verandah grouped about a village green, which is in turn dominated by the town hall from where 'the elect' once governed in magisterial fashion. It does give the towns an elegance lost in latter-day developments. In Boston, dignified brownstone townhouses co-exist with new shopping complexes created out of old town-halls. A booming trade with Europe formed the basis of Boston's former wealth. Now hi-tech industries, hospitals and universities are the big income earners, particularly hospitals. A qualified doctor — even if not in medicine — never admits his title to anyone in trade since it means an extra 50% on the bill. The smallest state in the Union boasts a splendid hospital as well as fashionable Brown University. Providence, Rhode Island's capital, has also been playing host to a trial of the island's truly rich in the von Bulow trial. Newport, where the alleged crime took place, is licking its wounds after losing both the America's Cup to the suddenly respected Australians, and the court case to Providence.

The woman judge sums up carefully what 'proved beyond all reasonable measure of doubt' means, what 'the taking of human life' can entail. She is scrupulous in her summary. Von Bülow shows a rare moment of humanity as he meets his dogs after a separation of years. His stepchildren snap at his heels just as they did in all those old fairy tales. The Americans have been no more successful than others in solving the basic human dilemmas. The very rich are revealed as no different from the rest of us — except that they have more money and can afford ruinously expensive litigation.

There's also a lot of poverty in Providence — long streets of old, run-down houses where you drive with your doors locked if you are a mid-American. The kids pick fights with the cops. You can always make a detour. But there are also the vast mansions out of which Jay Gatsby could walk at any minute, the shops and restaurants are open till late, the town is alive with strollers with time and money to spare.

New England is relaxed, with an easy way of life, if you have the entry ticket — cash.

'We come from New York, lived there for many years, till we got jobs in Providence. Yeah, it's a beautiful part of the country, great to bring the kids up in, you feel they're growing up with a better outlook on life somehow. But I do miss the buzz of a big city. Every few weeks I have to go to Boston, just to see the shops, theatres and art galleries — but it's still not New York.'

This is the world of the country club, where the professors' and surgeons' wives take their kids to swim and play tennis on summer afternoons. Another form of recreation is whale watching. A boat takes you from Plymouth Harbour out along the Massachusetts coast to spot the female hump-backed whales with their young. (Their mates take separate summer holidays in the Caribbean.) The passengers all rush to the side of the boat as a whale is spotted. 'Don't rock the boat,' implores the guide, 'we're here to study their habits, not to frighten them.'

On return, the tourists' films reveal vast expanses of ocean and minute patches of whale, but this distant encounter with the beauty of a huge intelligent beast stays longest of all impressions in easy, comfortable New England.

following page
Beachwood, former mansion of the Vanderbilts. The leading ladies of Newport, Rhode Island, used to vie with each other in the lavishness of their homes. It was the age of the great monopolist millionaires when the very few were very rich indeed. Today tourists are shown round by 'houseguests' wearing turn-of-the-century costume.

Hundreds of visitors a day visit Plymouth Plantation, Massachusetts with its reproduction Pilgrim village where animals are kept, herbs and vegetables are grown and actors assuming English accents carry out repair work on their wooden cottages.

It took the Americans nearly three centuries to push out from the original 13 colonies into the far West of the continent — occasioning the brutal Indian wars of the 1870's and the last defeat of the white man at Little Big Horn. Any serious attempt to understand the country must retread those old Indian trails, moving out from the early settlements into what was a largely unknown land. Fur trappers were usually the precursors of the great movements of people opening up the country.

Now there are highways where there were once sacred Indian trails. But the sheer sweep of the land means that even a little of the reverence for the earth and its creation will linger if a traveller allows himself to be at all influenced by the physical presence of the country. The first great divide comes with the Appalachian mountains that stand some several hundred miles back from the East Coast and stretch down its length. After the greenness of New York State the trees get steadily more populous as you climb up the great sweeping curves of road. Soon you are running parallel to the first of the Great Lakes, Lake Ontario. This lake receives a huge volume of water from the next lake along, Lake Erie, at the spot we know as Niagara Falls. A perpetual mist of spray hangs above the plunging fuming white waters as you look across to Canada and the North with its dark forests and isolated settlements dotted among the majesty of the tundra. For the Indians this was one of the most sacred spots of all, reached by a journey of many days over the forested hills. Watkins Glen. Now a motor racing circuit. A quarter Indian waitress serves me my meal, and is surprised at her antecedents being recognised.

Proceeding westwards through Pennsylvania you are surrounded by trees for almost the whole length of the state. The population is still 70% German in many areas, and like the country they came from, the state is clean and tidy, with the people attentive and polite without being effusive. The forests must make them feel at home. Next comes the 'buckeye' state — Ohio — and you enter the great plains that stretch down the centre of America in an unbroken extremely fertile flatness. The darkness of the soil tells you of its fertility and the ultimate reason for America's wealth. The openness of the land brings about a change in the character of the environment. Pennsylvania feels closed and secret. I am driving through a small town on the edge of the woods looking for a place to park the car. As I drive into the woods I notice that a pick-up truck is following at a distance. When you want to sleep in your car you don't advertise the fact. I pass from wide tracks to small tracks and finally park in a cul-de-sac hidden by tall trees. At two in the morning I look out the back window to see the lights of a pick-up truck passing slowly through the woods. They don't notice the turn I have taken. It passes like a dream. I remember my car has Canadian number plates, and it is a small town I came through.

But the woods are behind now. Ohio is the nation's third largest producer of grapes, any farmer can reap a rich harvest here. But along the shores of Lake Erie with the cities of Cleveland and Toledo and, just around the corner, Detroit in Michigan, you are more struck by the sprawl of the old heavy industries. The 'smokestack' industries that have been in long-term decline and were hit by the recession of the early 80s. Old warehouses decay by the polluted lake where uncounted quantities of industrial effluent were poured. In the days of industrial boom for these towns, the earth was seen as something to be tamed, not co-operated with. Steel and machines were lord. The cities themselves reflect the view that

A storm over Lake Erie, part of the system of five Great Lakes which straddle the border with Canada. Even though the great majority of Candians live within 100 miles of the USA, they have pursued a different foreign policy most notably when they played host to Vietnam War draft resisters. They also have a different, more relaxed lifestyle and a 'younger' mentality. Most noticeably of all, theirs is a spotlessly clean country with less division between the rich and poor.

page 38-39

Sunrise over one of the smaller lakes bordering Lake Erie in Ohio. The lakes have begun to be re-claimed from earlier widescale pollution as a greater appreciation of their uniqueness combines with a decline in the old heavy industries.

The American car manufacturers made over $10 billion in profits in 1984-5 as a result of belatedly catching up with the trends in design and petrol consumption. Their customers demand comfort first and performance second. Yet 1 in 3 vehicles sold are pick-up trucks. Americans like to move on, they move 14 times in a lifetime on average.

The borders of Pennsylvania and Ohio, thickly wooded hills intermingled with rivers. At the border with Ohio you come across Ukranian and Polish communities. Pennsylvania has been predominantly settled by German descent immigrants.

man had become subservient to his productions. The shapes are all gaunt and squat. Dirt and grime are deeply worked into the surface of the old factories.

The western edge of Pennsylvania sees the start of the change of racial mixture in the inhabitants. In Ohio you see many Poles and Ukranians, Toldeo people are rough hewn like their town and its industries. Still full of an energy that must express itself physically rather than in art or fashion or intellectual productions. A nuclear power station belches forth smoke from its huge chimney stack addding a new factor in the conundrum of pollution. The disregarding inhabitants live cheek by jowl with the new edifice as they have done with the old industrial behemoth constructions. They do realise that they must bring in more of the new labour-intensive industries if they are not permanently to be some of the first victims of any turndown in the economy.

The plains of America are the scene of some of its fiercest storms. Eerily — as the lake would suggest — a storm sweeps up, moving in a northerly direction from the Southwest. It is a more dramatic and extreme climate than the one the settlers left back in Europe two or three generations ago. Above Lake Erie are distant flashes of lightning which head, from my vantage point beside a small tributary lake, towards Toledo and then on to Chicago — the great market place and railhead for the producers of the plains.

Suddenly the rain is unleashed by the storm. The lightning flashes get closer, the thunderclaps louder. The highway is lit by these vivid electric blue flashes, distorting distance and perspective. Yet the great truck rigs thunder on. The deluge reaches a blinding intensity. The flashes of lightning come every few seconds. The world has been turned into a place more electrifyingly strange than anything a designer has so far imagined for a disco. The lights in front start flashing with a stroboscopic intensity. Great trucks could be hurtling up behind me as the man in front slows almost to a halt in the blinding downpour and then pulls frantically over to the side. Fortunately all the approaching traffic slows to a steady 10mph and the frightened bemused driver is left behind. Illuminated by the lightning the convoy proceeds. The plains are showing their earliest aspect as an untamed unfenced land (barbed wire fences were a great turning point for the American lifestyle). Here millions of bison wandered until they were slaughtered in an orgy of self-repeating-rifle madness in just 10 years. The tragedy of that massacre hangs heavy over the land till this day, it is the inheritance of those who have laid claim to the land with their boundary fences of sharpened metal.

Indiana and Illinois continue Ohio's unrelieved flatness. The black earth tells you of the richness of the soil. But before plunging out into cowboy country — the West — there is a grand metropolis upon Lake Michigan, namely Chicago. Here is a juxtaposition of decaying inner city tenements almost exclusively occupied by black people who came here from the South, and soaring office blocks next to the blue waters of the lake. A group of homosexual men cluster by the shore upon a hillock, girls walk their dogs or cycle by, but Chicago — in spite of its manifestations of late 20th century wealth — is still largely great marshalling yards for freight wagons, chimneys belching into the sky, great ironclad constructions that daunt the eye. The city dates from a time when men built their cities to impress with the monumental scale. The world has moved on, leaving Chicago a little behind. The poor state of the roads seems token of the poor state of the people's morale.

Beyond beckon the open spaces. There is a compulsion to press on, to leave behind the migrants who got as far as the great cities of Detroit and Michigan in their search for work and looked no further. In these surroundings beauty can get lost or mis-directed. I am photographing a girl sitting in a red Ford Mustang, she is fat, slumped lazily in her seat, munching her gum. I pull out my camera at the lights and shoot, a woman behind hoots, perhaps to warn the girl she is being photographed. Now the woman behind overtakes in her new Ford, and once having overtaken starts to look in her driver's mirror rearranging her hair, expecting she will get photographed. She is certainly better looking but in these parts charm, even in the good looking, has given way to competitiveness.

Out in the plains again. A man is preaching on the radio from Peoria. 'You have only to believe in Jesus Christ and you will be reborn. Not feel reborn. But be reborn. You have only to believe. It can happen to anyone. Doesn't have to be a person who observes regular churchgoing, can be anyone who believes.'

Jutson 'Woody' Ezzell does not believe. He is a stranger hereabouts. I pick him up near the biggest conventional arms depot in the country at Moline Island on the border with Iowa.

'Down in Florida and Carolina and in California there's a lot of partying. The folks in these parts they're strange.' he drawls in a soft low southern accent.

His line goes back almost to the time of the first settlements down in the South. He has the dark smouldering look of an Elvis Presley, a hint of 18th century buccaneer attitudes, to him these 'newcomers' from Poland, Germany, Sweden, Denmark, Italy, are not the true Americans who celebrate their good fortune. In a Nebraska township of 3,500 people — Gothenburg — he drawls to the barmaid. 'There's only two bars in this town? Any smoking go on? You tried cocaine? There's a lot of that in Florida.'

'I tried it when I was at college for a year in the Quad cities (on the borders of Iowa and Illinois) but I've settled down more now. I have a kid.'

The black ghetto area of Chicago. Like all large American cities, Chicago received a great influx of blacks from the South during the 20s and 30s as they came seeking work. Unlike their southern cousins, those in the big cities seem to have had a problem adapting to their new conditions. A homicide rate of 6 times that of the white population indicates a high level of rage and frustration.

The railroad crossing at Gothenburg, Nebraska, an agricultural town of 3,500 largely descended from Swedish immigrants. It is dawn but already a goods train over a mile long has thundered through and the pick-up truck is out on its business. Gothenburg is proud that their bank was one of the few in the area which did not fail in the Depression of the 30s. The small farmers are now in trouble across the nation because of the high value of the dollar.

'I have two,' Woody drawls.

He is on his way to California. He has a wife and two children aged one and two. Sometimes he likes his wife, sometimes not. He's heading West via Kentucky where his car broke down. He was once a motor mechanic, then a mirror hanger.

'There's money in that. I worked in apartments in Florida where two bedrooms will cost you $250,000 by the shore. In one block with 52 apartments only four people live there. The security's so strict no one can get in after five. One couple have owned their place for five years and still haven't been there. You should go to Florida or New Orleans or California. The women are more open, not like up here. I have a house in California, I work as a male dancer now, did some body building some three years ago. You can earn $1,000 to $2,000 a week. The women will try and touch you, put some money in your pouch. I just love to dance, that heavy beat, they chase after you, they're just aren't as many women around up here.'

Out of the windows it's Nebraska, and there are only cows in pens being worked by a solitary cowboy on his horse. This is cowboy country at last. There's a sign indicating the way to Boot Hill. Back in Illinois there was a sign pointing to Ronald Reagan's birthplace, N W Illinois. Flat open land with a sense of boundless possibilities perhaps, but unvaried. Here it's hilly. 20 miles from Reagan's birthplace an 82-year-old man comes in the local restaurant. Upright, well in control of his faculties. He's down from Wisconsin with his daughter. He pulls out a newspaper clipping.

'The day Mendota beat the Harlem Globetrotters. It's from 57 years ago. Six of that Mendota team are still alive,' Chuck says. 'I have everything I want, a garden, I grow some strawberries. Smoke the occasional cigar. The doctor, he told me to leave cigarettes alone. Cigarettes is death. We only lost two games out of 27 that year,' says the veteran survivor, sure he has found his place in the sun.

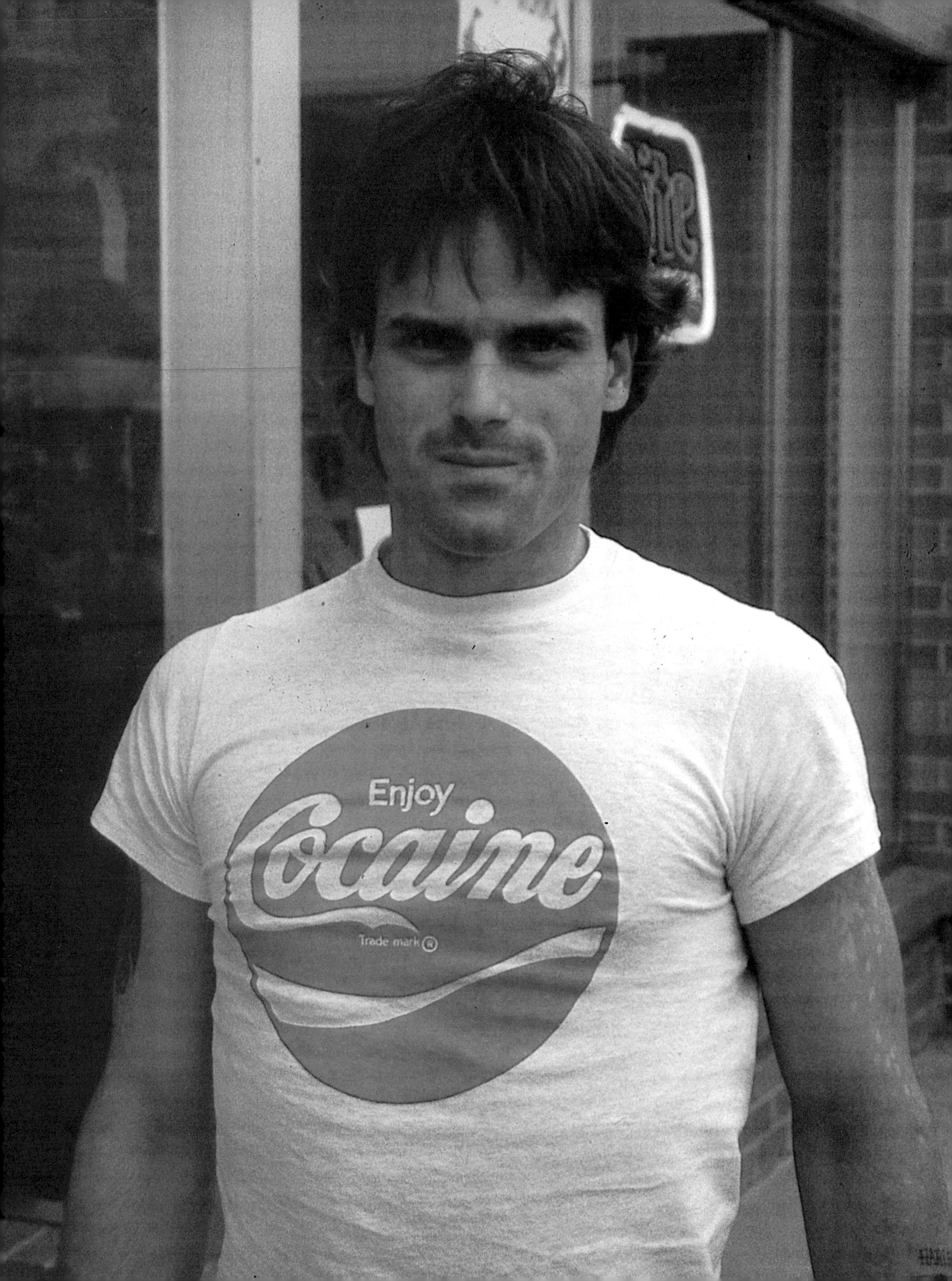
Enjoy
Cocaine
Trade mark ®

'This is a storm warning. A tornado has been reported at 8.10pm in the Grand Island area. It is moving NE at approximately 35mph. Go immediately to a room with no windows — a cellar, a bathroom, or a room in the middle of the house. Lie down flat and cover your head with a blanket. Do not wait to close any doors or windows. I repeat the National Weather Service has issued a tornado warning up till 8.25pm. Stop whatever you are doing and take shelter. Do not look out of doors, serious injury can come from flying glass.'

The message comes over the car radio, the rain, already heavy, becomes intense. The truck up ahead continues as the announcer issues the warning with a sharp urgency to his voice. A town nearby here in NE Nebraska was hit by 7 tornadoes in one year, destroying much of the area. The local people take the warning seriously enough. Woody Ezzell and I pass cars pulled in to the side of the road with their hazard lights flashing in the extraordinarily heavy rain. Then the truck in front pulls over, a signal if ever there was one, that we must be in the danger area. We have just passed a line of cars huddled under a highway bridge where it looks extremely dangerous to be parked if the big trucks are still driving on. There is a car which has dived into the central reservation so that it is halfway down the dip with its tail jutting out. The truck and ourselves come to a stop some 50 yards past the bridge, we are on a raised embankment. Suddenly the wind is blowing the rain into a white fury of water that is driven across the road. The car rocks under the force of this wind. I suggest to Woody that perhaps we'd be better off in the dip of the central reservation. The radio repeats its warning.

'The most dangerous place to be right now is in a mobile home or a car on the highway.'

Not very reassuring to hear as the world outside the car window becomes a seething white-tossed mass of water with visibility lost in grey swirl. Just as suddenly as it started the wind dies down. We can see to the other side of the road. The radio comes on again to say that the tornado has been reported in our area at 8.20pm. 15 minutes later the sky is clear, the sun is setting, there are great sheets of water flooding the fields. Tornadoes touch down very suddenly.

'There has been an confirmed report of tornado touchdown at 8.20pm,' the radio says. It is 8.35pm.

'The storm is moving in a NE direction at 35mph. The alert has been extended to 9.15pm.'

Opposite page

Jutson 'Woody' Ezzell far from his Carolina home, in the heart of the mid-West. He regards the people as 'Johnnies come lately' since his ancestors arrived here over two hundred years ago. His is a more relaxed lifestyle, sure that the huge land will provide for him. He's probably right.

Previous page

The lakeside in downtown Chicago. A recreation area for the whole town with picnics and parties, joggers, sunbathers, sailors, ice cream salesman, couples, gays.. in fact the whole gamut of the city's population.

Rebecca and Linda are reunited after a year. Big hugs on the doorstep of the little town house teeming with houseplants. Linda — a singer — has spent a year in London and has now returned to Denver. The girls have arranged to go out to dinner and then go see Julie, who is a mutual friend, perform at one of Denver's prestige night clubs. She will have a Brazilian backing group.

Rebecca is 34, a fast-talking shrewd lady originally from Michigan. She's been in Denver 12 years, plays harmonica three times a week with a group.

'A year ago I had to decide whether to go off travelling around on gigs with them. But I'm 34, I don't have that much energy any more for running two full-scale careers (she also works in advertising). Besides, my friends, my support network, are here. I decided to stay. We play reggae type music. No, you can't support yourself just on playing music in Denver. We're looking for a new drummer, the one we have is great but he plays with another band and we get put second. After a year of playing together we've built up an understanding. I just rehearse three evenings a week, that's enough for me together with the job.'

The club Julie is playing is The Chrysler. We reach there circuitously after a Mongolian meal in a smart — not to say chic — restaurant with pink walls. The club's on the fourth floor of a sparklingly new building in downtown Denver. We are ushered to a table in ultra-smart surroundings. The clientele is impeccably dressed in fashionable casual wear. There are many groups of men and women sprinkled with a minority of couples. Julie is standing beside the microphone. Blonde hair. Fresh face. She could pass for 25 but is actually 30. The band consists of a black drummer, who plays on large drums with his palms and fingers accompanied by two guitarists, one of whom is swarthily Portuguese while the other is more Indian-looking and sensitive.

Julie wears a black full dress, puffed out at the shoulders. The back is cut low with an intricate design threading across the white flesh. She could be a younger version of Peggy Lee — and sings a little like that.

The waitress solicitously asks what drinks we would like. Ten minutes later she has returned to ask if there's anything else we'd like. She takes the refusal graciously.

By this time Julie is singing, head held back, eyes closed, sighing into the microphone. The highly professional performance is largely lost on the clientele who are gently chattering.

She finishes her set, comes to sit down at the table. Smiles ecstatically. We have been transported to the softer warmer climes of South America, not very far you reflect, thinking of the size of the continent. And if Julie is to reach the heights she will have to move south and west to Los Angeles or north and east to New York. She looks content to be the queen for the night. The waitress asks me to total the bill. She means add her tip. It's all done very smoothly. They don't miss too much in Denver where you can sense the oil money, the military money, the tourist money. It does wonders for the people's morale.

Linda, only a week back from London, takes me to Red Rock. A natural amphitheatre where ancient, intricately-worn red rocks make a perfect auditorium from which to look out over a long valley.

'One day I shall sing here,' says Linda. 'The Grateful Dead are playing here next week. The concerts are sold out.'

We pass two women who could be Indians, with their sensual lips and silky dark hair. You can hardly fail to be aware that this is an ancient sacred site.

Previous page

Birds fly against the backdrop of a sunset 20 miles from President Reagan's birthplace in NW Illinois. It is rich farming country with some early history of being the route the pioneers took on their progress westward.

The Rockies stretch away from under a magnificent open sky in Colorado. With only three million inhabitants — many of them newly arrived — the impact of oil, tourist and military money has produced a sense of a land just being opened up, as much of it undoubtedly is.

In Gothenburg, Nebraska, is a monument set up to commemorate the famous but short-lived Pony Express. This operation, with riders who were almost still boys, cut the journey time of letters from the towns of the plains to the Pacific Coast down to 10 days. It lasted from 1860-61, lost 100,000 dollars(in that era's money) and the lives of many men who manned the staging points where the riders could change horses. They were targets for the Indians, the riders did rather better in the mortality stakes. The monument says it is dedicated to all those pioneers who pass this way on the Oregon Trail opening up the West. Gothenburg, as its name implies, is largely peopled by Scandinavian-Americans, they have prospered from the soil and boast of having the only bank in the area which did not go under in the Great Depression.

In the mythology of America, this land is still the frontier. Certainly the West has wide-open, sparsely populated spaces. I walk into a store in Walsenburg, Colorado, and am confronted by an old man with two rows of teeth and a wife who looks decidedly simple. The store's goods lie in marvellous disarray surveyed by an elk's head.

You start to see the cowboys in western Nebraska, one or two men working great herds of cattle. North and South Dakota, Wyoming, Arizona, Colorado... all along the Rockies you'll find the cowboy is alive and well. Signs dot the road announcing who passed through before. I'm at Fort Garland, Kit Carson's old command on the Navajo trail passing just above New Mexico where there are large Indian reservations. Later I pass Commanche national grasslands in New Mexico, flat mountain plains broken only by mountains that surge out of the earth. In the twilight some of these mountains take on a man-made shape like that of a pyramid — and indeed there are confirmed Aztec ruins in New Mexico near Cedar Hill.

The wide open country continues as I head towards Texas. At Clayton there are two mountains that probe above the flat land. The locals call them Rabbit Ears after an Indian chief who fought a ferocious battle with the white man in 1856. In Clayton the cowboys 'wear chaps because otherwise the cactus would tear up their legs,' my host for the night — Joe Kelley of the Mission Motel — informs me. 'All the land's owned by the big corporations now. The cowboys don't herd the cattle, big transporters take them to market.'

The entirely flat plains of the Mid West are suddenly interrupted by the sky scrapers of a town, in this case Lincoln, Nebraska.

following page
The Sangre de Cristo Mountains in Colorado near the border with New Mexico with Mt Blanca rising to over 14,000 feet. The old Navajo trail ridden by Kit Carson leads on to Navajo Indian reservations in Utah and Arizona, while beyond lies California.

I enter The Roadrunner lounge in dusty Main Street. It's a country and western band onstage. The lead singer is calling out the tunes as the men, who have taken off their spurs and hats in deference to the ladies, skip and dance their way around the floor. There are all ages here celebrating Carl's birthday. A big young man in a straw cowboy hat hugs a tiny wisp of a woman who seems to have been worn away by hard work.

'Hello Momma,' he cries, friendly like. Then his two equally large friends hug momma as well. The men make up an unconscious high fashion parade, for they have all the details right, unlike the parodists in downtown Manhattan. There's button-down shirts with many pockets and buttons. Blue jeans. Clonking leather boots. Magnificent hats of every shade. A lot of the older men seem to have limps. From falling off horses? But there are younger ones, ready to take their places, who know all the old steps and all the old tunes. The atmosphere is cosy and warm, boisterous and self-contained at the same time. Yet these people will listen attentively to the pristinely clad, enormously rich Barbara Walters on ABC News. America is big enough to have many variations on its aspirational theme. The women, the younger ones anyway, are also dressed in jeans and ornamented shirts, most are already getting fat.

Joe Kelley tells me that he was in Australia in the war. 'Now that's pioneer country still, like we used to be. I reckon they'll find lots of minerals there, it's the place with the opportunities now.' His cowboy neighbours look as though they are doing nicely thank you. Here they drive big pick-up and big limos. In fact, a third of Americans drive pick-ups, a lot still hanker for the range.

50 miles to the west of Denver you are in an old mining area, with a still flourishing tradition of independence. It's backwoodsmen country where the old American West of myth most closely matches the reality.

The local coffee shop in Walsenburg, Colorado, with Elaine as your host. You're in the authentic American Wild West here, Walsenburg has the atmosphere of an old forgotten cowboy town. Behind Elaine is an example of Oklahoma folk art, a male bird preens itself before a female.

Where is the frontier today? I wonder, thinking back to that drive out from Denver 45 miles to the west in the mountains. We stopped at a roadside bar. A complete contrast to Denver where the oil wealth from exploration companies is rivalling that of Texas and California. The men were long-haired and check-shirted, lounging at tables drinking beer. They were different from the cowboys of Clayton as well as the well-dressed city people. Backwoodsmen you'd call them, another old American tradition. Though many of these people are still forgetting the Vietnam War and the freedom that went with it for those who threw off the government draft yoke. It's still pioneer country. 50 years ago they were mining lead around here, and there were very few people. 200 miles south and the land opens up into great tracts that are still undeveloped. Forbes magazine is selling off 5-acre tracts to 'Americans who want to have a stake in the frontier wilderness'. It's a dream of course. But half a dozen of the 'ranch' owners have built their wooden houses to survey the wild mountains. I am looking down at a pass that the pioneers drove through on their way further west. My guide is part Indian. You feel the invasion of privacy the settlers represented, even today. I notice the great sweep of the semi-arid lands of New Mexico to the south, dotted with clumps of jutting rock formations familiar from so many cowboy films. I notice the snow-covered mountain in the distance, and feel its extreme beauty. My guide has a reverence for the land just like his Indian ancestors (whom he shares with French and Spanish blood lines). He must find it strange that anyone should want to 'own' a small tract of land when all of it is here for everyone to enjoy. But the Indians never did understand how the white man imagined he could possess the earth. They have thousand of years experience of its ways, that is their true possession, one day the white man will have to learn that wisdom. The mountain peak glistens in the sun, white blue and charcoal against a stormy sky. My Indian guide half smiles, he pretends to know very little, but all the time he is eagle eyed and fully awake to every contour of the land.

# SHOW ME THE WAY TO AMARILLO

**13**

The Texas panhandle is flat and wide to the horizon — the people have a commensurate sense of a broad open future. The terrible ravages of the 1930s droughts which produced a dustbowl, have been replaced by a whiff of oil money. True the oil derricks are not producing quite the fortune they were before but Texas is still a state with no local taxes which means that even the film companies are now setting up studios here in an effort to cut costs. The contrast with the neighbour state of Oklahoma is instructive.

Even though Oklahoma was the last state to be opened up in the dying days of the last century, it has a lazy air about it like much of the old South. (Dieticians are now ascribing this laziness to an inadequate intake of vitamins and proteins, both among the blacks and the poor whites). The people you see in the bars and restaurants fit the description of redneck well. They're old English stock not built for the rigours of the southern sun. Over several centuries they have gradually moved west in search of land and opportunity — two perennial American preoccupations. The faces have a knowledge of the land worn into them, creased tanned and weather beaten as they are.

Oklahoma becomes steadily more arboreal the further east you travel. Hills begin to break up the flat plains of eastern Texas, it is arable farming country. The next state, Arkansas, has an even firmer rooting in the past. You're in the Deep South, where the majority of America's black people still live in spite of the mass migrations to the North in the 20s and 30s. Its capital — Little Rock — which was desegregated in the late 50s after a well-reported clash between the local people and the Federal marines, has returned to its accustomed 'backwater' slowness. But Little Rock, situated on the mighty Mississippi, dividing the old and the new America, is not the ultimate backwater in the middle of the great continent. That prize could go to Fort Smith on the borders with Oklahoma. It's an embodiment of an old American joke, 'If it's fun, they ban it in Arkansas.'

Fort Smith in the evening about 10pm. A few cars prowl the main street driven by attractive girls with nowhere to go. The cars, like the women, are sleek. They overtake you, with the drivers looking neither to left or to right, lost in some dream of their worth.

There is only one bar open in the town and that is tucked away off Main Street. The barman snorts and snarls at his customers — who include a very large black lady with notable biceps, a cripple in a wheel chair, a woman with a weathered face wearing blouse and jeans who is in her late 30s, three or four rather crusty men, and a beefy man in his late 30s who is arm wrestling the black woman and narrowly wins. Empty futility hangs in the air. Outside the streets offer but one attraction — four stores selling water beds.

It is almost as if time has stopped still in the bar. You could — allowing for the different dress — be back in the 18th century in some tavern where the level of communication extends to a belly laugh and a bellow. There has been little incentive for progress since the South was defeated in the Civil War.

*Previous page*

A grizzly bear shot in the Rockies. They are still to be found both in the big parks like the Yellowstone and in the immense woods of the North West where there have been persistent rumours of ape-like men being sighted.

*Opposite page*

In the South, the old certitudes still hold sway and by the time this boy is grown up you can be sure that those old values will be remarkably intact.

*following page*

Little Rock, Arkansas, became known for its refusal to desegregate a school in the 50s. Today, there's little sign of blatant racial segregation. By the time these two urban cowboys grow up you may find the South has leapt ahead of the North in its treatment of the black population.

However, in Little Rock you'll find an unconscious but more real integration of the races than in the North where the ghettos still predominate. For one thing, the blacks are a higher proportion of the population in the South. A white woman sits down on the same bench at the bus station as two black women. Underneath, the two races understand each other well, and are rooted in a long shared history. It is the North which is now having the greatest difficulty coming to terms with the black population, for up there the southern negroes have lost their roots. The South has very slowly evolving customs to fall back upon.

Moving on into Tennessee, you see the successful blacks in the latest cars, mixing with their peers on terms of rough equality, unlike Britain for example, where they are simply ignored. The rich farmland of Tennessee has been worked for two centuries. The first settlers moving out west from Virginia along the James River, found rivers teeming with fish, plentiful game, thick woods, and rich pasture. There are stories of the prolificacy of the land before the white man came. Great flights of ducks, seven miles long, whose numbers blotted out the sun, herds of bison numbering millons, even after three centuries there is still a lot of wildlife left. This sense of a found and now lost paradise stays with the descendants of the pioneers. The people feel little need to look out to the world beyond their shores. The farms produce a rich harvest with a surplus more often than not. It shows in the girth of the people. There has been relatively little later immigration into the state so that many of the old ways are preserved. A courteous approach to strangers, a deeply felt reverence for Baptist teachings, many born-again Christians ready to praise the Lord for their good fortune.

History and continuity permeate the South, for it has a long history even by European standards. This woman hurrying through the rain would not have looked out of place 100 years ago. She belongs.

**14** It could be Gabby Hayes I'm talking to. He has the same drawl. And a damned hornery fella he could be if you crossed him. But he likes the music in the bar. He starts telling me about the man further down the bar counter.

'That's George Jones, he wrote the song the band are singing, A Girl I Used to Know.'

It's a real Western bar, long and made of very solid wood. George (like Gabby) is in full cowboy gear. George's shirt is all long tassles, white against the black cloth, but you'd expect that from a big country and western star. Matter of fact, my eyes were drawn to him before I knew of his claim to fame in the 'music capital of the world.' George has got a sad but sharp, serious but wise face. He is melancholy in his cups, but then so are most country songs. He trips out the doorway with its chest-high swing doors as they play his most famous song. He raises a hand in acknowledgement. On to another bar. Gabby meanwhile is falling asleep.

'That's how I get with the drink,' he says with a start. He shows me his hands. Rough hands.

'I'm a working man. Work with steel. My wife's a cousin of Brenda Lee. You know King of the Road? That was written by Roger Miller about the street out there, Broadway, the centre of Nashville.'

Innocent looking black hookers wait on one of its corners. A very large black man, with matching muscles, bare chested under his tiny waistcoat, is framed in the doorway. He wears a black hat to set off his black clothes. At least a third of the original cowboys were black or Mexican.

The band were famous, I discover, back in about 49. 'All the best music's made here,' says Gabby. 'Here have this drink. It's not open. Can't drink anymore.'

Ten minutes later he is joining me in another beer. Two men, as colourful as peacocks in their cowboy gear, are dancing with two women. One of the women is small and plain, the other heavy and ageing. Brown hens in comparison. The barmaid smiles tensely as Gabby begins to nod off on his seat again. The barman jabs him awake.

Gabby Hayes in reflective mood in Nashville, Tennessee, one night when George Jones shared the same bar and the band played his hit 'A Girl I Used To Know.' Sad, maudlin, full of the homespun virtues, that's Nashville music and maybe heartland America's.

The singer and his guitarist are joined by Lee Anderson, who's got a neck as thick as a bull's, whose bloated frame nevertheless looks strong. Two cowboys, dressed in white from head to toe, pause at the doorway. You wait for the film director to shout 'action'. But it's the same at the next bar, and the next. All those songs you've heard were modelled on characters like these, in the home of the Gran' Ol Opry.

'When did that start?' I ask Gabby.

'Damned if I know, years ago,' says Gabby, rubbing his grey beard in bemusement.

'When did the Gran' Ol Opry start?' he asks the barman.

'1932 or 33 was it?' he volunteers after a moment's thought. He has a huge beer gut, permanently chews on a tooth pick.

The road to Nashville passes the Loretta Lynn Dude Ranch, 80 miles west of the town. Some people make it big, though the film of her life 'The Coalminer's Daughter' plainly established that it wasn't an easy passage. It's Fan Fair Week and folks from places like Pittsburg, Pennsylvania, are in town. In authentic jeans, both men and women, though the men are inevitably paunchy now, and the women also running to fat. Their prime was in the early 50s, they're reliving the old simpler days. However, the cowboy tradition lives manfully on. I watch the rodeo stars on the TV and see the world champion rise to speak in the microphone as he receives his award. He is clean cut and neat, thanks his mom and dad for all they've done for him. He's from North Dakota, not for him will the streets of Nashville have any great appeal. Why there's a strip show across from the Rheingold Cowboy bar, and the black hookers, who giggle good-humouredly. Nashville retains a faded innocence. All those songs about girls, a lonely life is that of a cowboy.

Previous page

The James River, Virginia. It was at the mouth of this river that the first settlers of America set up home nearly 400 years ago. Gradually the settlers were lured along the river by the promise of plenty from the land. But it took nearly 50 years for them to make much headway. From then on, Americans have never looked back.

The Shenandoah Hills, Virginia, little more than a 100 miles from Washington DC but the pace is altogether that of an older, more peaceful America. The settlers came lured by tales of paradise on earth... it is a search that has never really ended.

Moon Rock displayed at the NASA Research Laboratory and Test Site on the border of Mississippi and Louisiana off I10. Manned flights to Mars are planned by the end of the century and there are several projects in operation aimed at making radio contact with extraterrestial civilisations. The odds are that we are not alone, but hardly anyone has realised the implications of this for our fragile egos. We could be about to find out.

Was it men like the rodeo champion who drove remorselessly onwards as they opened up the wooded hills with their lakes and streams and teeming wildlife? Or was it men like Thomas Flatman? In neighbouring Oklahoma there's a plaque in his hometown proudly proclaiming that he was one of NASA's first spacemen.

Just outside Washington DC on the way to the airport in Baltimore you'll find the NASA Goddard Center. In rural-America surroundings that have changed little since the 18th century you'll find one of the centers where the conquest of space is being mapped out. The people have found a new frontier to aim for. These riders of the space machines have the same laconic acceptance and humility as their cowboy predecessors.

I meet another embodiment of the ideal. Brian, hitching back up the coast after 18 months in Texas working as a miner. 'When I came through here (the Virginia Hills) they were high with snow,' he says. He calls out to the girls in downtown Roanoke, Virginia. One blows back a kiss. He is wild with the knowledge of all that is possible in this vast country, hardly yet fully exploited or aware of its strengths.

Not so long ago Atlanta, heart of the Confederacy, again became the centre of attention for America as a peanut farmer won the presidency on the strength of a campaign that relentlessly attacked the Federal government and its corrupts ways. Coming from the depressed South where the hurts of the Civil War still lingered in a tangible way, Carter well understood the need to bring reconciliation to a bitterly divided nation. The rolling Appalachian mountains that take you from Tennessee to Georgia's capital are still settled and undisturbed by the outside world, it is the old America. On the corner of Virginia, I find a petrol station where the plastic credit card is still unknown. The attendant — in a slow drawl — takes his time redirecting me. This old steady rhythm is again making itself felt through the country. Once again America can see itself as a defender of freedom. The man who set this in motion, Carter, what kind of a state did he come from? I ring Plains and ask for Jimmy Carter's phone number. Immediately a recorded message gives me his office number. Computerisation has reached down into a South that has become one of the most rapidly growing areas in the country. A polite friendly voice answers.

'Thank you for your call, sir. You should speak to Toni Baker, President Carter's press officer.'

above

General Sherman's infamous march to the sea from Atlanta destroyed much of the old South. But in Macon, further south, you can see examples of ante-bellum artchitecture. 'The South will rise again,' was the final defiant cry as the old elegance was swept away.

Previous page

A magnificent example of the true American car, owned by John Kelley of the Mission Motel, Clayton, New Mexico. He receives Christmas cards from all over the world . Many of his visitors are from Colorado Springs, a big military center.

The Deep South was very pleased to have a President after more than 100 years in the wilderness. In these parts, it is as if he is still President. While George Wallace, victim of assassin's gun in the early 70s, is in actuality still Governor of Alabama. I examine the local paper in Riverside, L.A. Big geese that look like turkeys paddle in the lake as a grey dawn comes up over the trees. It's February, but you can easily imagine the lush vegetation in the height of humid summer. Last night I was listening to frogs clicking away like unwinding clockwork springs as the rain hammered down on the car roof. Last week, the northern part of Alabama was frozen up in the worst snows for 20 years as a storm moved up the Tennessee Valley.

George Wallace is busy pronouncing. It's 'seat belt month'. Pregnant women should ensure that the lap belt is under the baby. 1 in 14 passengers are probably pregnant. He regrets that outside government rulings have overturned the punishment of death for rape 'which we all remember as the traditional punishment.' However, he has successfully overturned a statue of limitations so that a rapist could be prosecuted when the law forces caught up with him after more than three years. He calls on individuals and private enterprises to come forward with spare generators after the snow has cut off towns in the north of the state and left them without electricity. George is still omnipresent in Alabama, nursing his people as his wife nurses him. There's an item on the news. A man has smashed 10 shopfront windows so that he would be placed in the cells. He wants to get near a man who has killed his 14-year-old son. The commentator adds that the father has not been allowed near the man. There has been hardly any crime in Riverside, however, in the last month. Just four arrests for minor infringements. Here is a part of America that lives by the old certitudes. The people are 90% Baptist with a smattering of Catholics, Methodists and Seventh Day Adventists. They are the descendants of English non-Conformists who came seeking religious freedoms. They have kept to the old ways far more closely than the people they left behind in Britain, who are now a distinct minority with a faith subverted into a caring form of politics, itself under threat in the economically troubled Britain of the 80s.

Rugged individualism is still the philosophy of the people here. 'You must have faith,' declares a woman in the bar, while the barmaid solicitously looks after her regular customers.

'I've worked just about everywhere around here,' she confides. There aren't that many places to work, you reflect. But the new wealth of the Reagan boom is filtering through to the South. The people's clothes are new, moderately priced and reasonably styled. The local radio is offering club membership for singles 'where the emphasis is on self-improvement. Cocktail parties, wine tasting, theatre outings...' Wealth brings an accompanying desire for a greater appreciation of the 'good things in life.'

'I loved that silk underwear in Marks and Spencers,' drools the air hostess to her friends. The southern belles like to be smartly turned out, theirs is an old tradition of gracious living that they are working to revive as the South finally shakes off a hundred years in the doldrums.

First job of the day is to ring Toni Brown. A very efficient – if probing – man screens the call. Mention of the project ensures I get through. 'He's out of the country most of the next week sir, it's a little short notice.'

I suggest I write.

'Where are you?'

'In Alabama heading for Dallas.'

The DJ in Birmingham, Alabama is canvassing for the local football bowl to be named after Bear Bryant, a football coach with a national name. 'Alabama had a negative image some 20 years ago (it fought long and hard against integrated buses) this man could help give Alabama a positive image — internationally.'

The DJ is from Tennessee, it seems he can afford to say Wallace is not universally loved. In the paper Governor Wallace is calling for the death penalty for drug traffickers. They have been finding it too hot in Florida and are now smuggling thousands of dollars worth of drugs into the Gulf states every day.

In the South, national politics has a different aspect from that in the North. It is the day of the State of the Union message from the real president, Ronald Reagan. Having seen the limitless plains he comes from, it's no surprise to hear him say that the only impediments put on people are those they impose on themselves. In the Baptist South you can see why he appeals across the broad swath of voters, in spite of the strong Democrat tradition. His appeal is visionary — 'there is nothing that faith, will and heart cannot achieve.'

The economic boom has not touched the run-down wooden houses that litter Highway 80 heading west. There are almost as many rusting old cars lying scattered on the edge of the highway as there are new ones upon it. A sign denotes the site of a Civil War battle, Grant's Canal at Vicksburg. The Union Army in 1862-3 press-ganged negro units into building a massive canal to bypass Confederate forces on the line of the Mississippi. The sign finishes with the message that Confederate artillery fire flooded the whole of the Union forces position, after it breached a dam holding back the water from the new canal. The Union has been having its revenge for much of the time since.

Forests surround the straight-as-an-arrow road through Alabama and Mississippi. Hawks hover overhead as you plunge further west. I stop off at a town called, appropriately, Forest, and strike up a conversation with a man whose leathery face proclaims more than a passing interest in the fact that 'it's getting warmer.'

The newspaper weather forecasts reveal bands of warmth the further south you get. From 0 degrees Fahrenheit on the Canadian border it slowly rises into the 40s in the South, while Florida is atypically enjoying temperatures that range from the 60s to the 80s down in Key West and Miami. Sticking outwards from the continental body like a priapic pleasure appendage Florida is attracting many of the country's retired.

'I remember 50 years ago, there was hardly a car to be seen. There's still more beef cattle in Florida than in Texas,' my informant tells me. 'I've been 6 years here in Mississippi but I'm going back. It's mean here, one day in the 30s, next day the 50s, then it's back to freezing again.'

I ask him how long his family have been in the States.

'Not sure that I know. Two hundred and more years.' I take in the extraordinary face. Extremely large ears, large nose. As though he is either an exotic mix of his antecedents or a rather particular type. But the eyes are Indian eyes, he belongs to the land, to the country. In contrast, the man passing with a feather in his hat unmistakably has German ancestry.

'Are there a lot of French around here?' I ask.

'No.'

I notice the bayous, the riverways, all have French names. He tells me that they still speak some French further south in Baton Rouge. You sense he regrets the influx of foreigners, the refugees from the colder states. In his time scale, this is all very recent.

'There's a lot of Indians in Florida down the east coast... and the west coast too...' he concludes.

For him all the inhabitants of the hamburger bar, including the black people who serve behind the counter, are recent arrivals. He is almost whispering as he waxes lyrical about the golden lobsters found off Key West. The fruits. The vegetables. The plenty that Florida produces. It does seem a miracle caught in the blasts of winter even this far south.

I take a road to a wildlife reserve. No sign of life among the melting snows. At the Mississippi River I walk back from where I finally manage to park the car. The white snows from further north are being swept along on the rapidly moving current. A small boat battles upstream. The frozen interior is carried to the warm Gulf before your eyes. The sheer size of the river is a shock, it is a mighty continental river, speaking of a north that is even yet hardly known as it turns to arctic wastes.

Hankering after Florida on a cold day in Mississippi, my informant paints a picture of a blessed agricultural state full of nature's bounty. As he talks of Key West and the islands he becomes positively ecsastic.

# DALLAS, OIL AND INSURANCE MONEY

I can't help liking the man in the cowboy hat and leather jacket who is leaning down through the car window, fixing me with a probing smile and pointing out that as well as driving on the wrong side of the road, Texans also have speed limits. He lets me off with a caution.

'You had a nice guy,' says my hitchhiker companion who spent the night outside in a below-freezing temperature and is only slowly thawing out. He sings to the country songs on the radio. John Denver singing Country Road in particualr, another of those poets of America who find romance in its vast distances and embracing landmass. The hitchhiker becomes a little more animated at the truck shop where the waitress has that indefinable but very apparent air of independence about her that belongs to the West. Perhaps it's just the hot black coffee. He's heading for Phoenix, Arizona.

'900 miles. That's a long way.'

I probe further. Does he think he might reach there before Sunday now, after his express lift from me?

'It's hard hitching out of Dallas,' he mutters.

He has no money, having lost 32 dollars during a truck ride.

'It probably fell out of my back pocket.'

He returns to contemplating the length of his journey. The country we pass through is increasingly opening out. Less pine forests, more rolling plains, the road stretching away into the blue murk. The light is bright and clear, although snow on the ground in the woods testifies to the cold outside. In the car it's warm and cosy, the music keeps on coming. Before too long I am dropping him off on the ring road that encircles Dallas.

'Now you have a good time in Florida,' he says on parting, his slicked down hair, wide eyes and stubble belieing the way he has his wits about him, as he must negotiating the intercrossing expressways with trucks thundering by. The traffic is fast, no one on the four lanes of the expressways is doing less than 60mph. A car abandoned on the hard shoulder is submerged in a murky grey dirt as if it is the frozen survivor from an earlier age, ignored by its latter-day descendants. The roads, I finally realise, have been gritted and the winds are showering this blanket of dust over everyone and everything.

Construction sites litter the roadside. Cranes dot the horizon, the soaring tower blocks in the center of town come into view. Away from the center in the suburb of Richardson, the houses spread out — single storey buildings made of wood. Newer 'condos now available for letting'. It's very obviously a boom town, (1,000 people a day are moving in), the wealth is founded on oil and insurance money that is being reinvested in new industries. Downtown there's a cleared building site, where a graphic picture of a soaring 40-storey high skyscraper and a sign announce that by Spring 87 it will be open. In Spring 85 the foundations have yet to be laid.

'Why don't you head down to Brownsville (near Mexico) on the Gulf? It's warm down there,' says my distributor, Tom Brown when I tell him I'm heading for Florida. Texas, bigger than France, offers a whole range of climates. Later he warms to the discussion of the Cajuns in Louisiana who speak the King's French (the King being Louis XIV). There was a time when the French held sway all along the Mississippi which was then known as the Louisiana territory. 'Life's slow around Baton Rouge, it's getting very pricey in New Orleans though.'

Previous page

The exponential growth rate of Dallas has thrown up a bewildering assortment of buildings, signs and public utilities. There is a piercing quality to the light in this town — which has no natural advantages — but has still contrived to become one of the most dynamic in America.

The illuminated sign of Pegasus — symbol of the Magnolia Oil Company — used to dominate the Dallas skyline. But an immigration rate of 1,000 people a day has created a new larger town around the old one.

Tom is Texan down to his big Western boots, his gold-ringed fingers and his pearl-studded belt. His mother remembers the carpet baggers who came down with their 'carpet bags' full of dubiously made goods at the end of the Civil War. Their exploitation of a prostrated local population is still bitterly remembered in the folklore. Originally the Browns, and his mother's side of the Phillips, hailed from Tennessee, but they were here in Texas by the 1850s. After the Alamo, before the Civil War. The White Plaza's hotel bar where we are sitting is the oldest in town. 60 years old.

'You can always tell by the size of the lobby, how grand a hotel was,' Tom comments.

The cowboy past has given way to an equally explosive present with every building that has not got a preservation order on it in danger of being redeveloped. The School Depository looms out of the black night next to the Kennedy Memorial.

'He was just a lone nut,' says Tom, rejecting all the conspiracy theories that have fuelled the media.

'What about LBJ, didn't he have a lot to gain from it? This is his country'. 'He wouldn't have organised it that messy way,' Tom replies. 'Now down in the basement of the Municipal Buildings is where Jack Ruby shot Oswald.'

'What happened to him, I forget.'

'He died of cancer a few months later. He was a nightclub owner with a high opinion of himself. Wanted to make a name for himself. He had advanced cancer, could have affected his brain.'

'Maybe he knew he didn't have long to go.'

'Maybe.'

The B&J Oyster Bar serves up fresh oysters... really fresh... neatly set in their shells surrounded by lots of ice. 'These would've been in the Gulf last night.' They are pinkly succulent. 'Any month there's an 'r' in it is good for oysters. The cold weather makes them lean and tough again, they get lazy and soft in the summer.'

The old building that dates from just after the Civil War resounds with the chatter of the people who have to queue to get a seat. The young men and women still have that lean 'get up and go' look, even though there's now a Dallas ballet. The windy downtown streets are walked by poor blacks.

# AS BIG AS TEXAS

Driving down a road that passes newly built, single storey homes. The road is so newly opened that the shops are advertising on handwritten billboards. The road becomes a dirt track. I pass 'keep out' signs, newly printed. Then more ominous signs saying 'Posted. Trespassing is an offence.' Finally, the dirt track gives out at a gate warning that past here is 'Private property.' Having just been passed on the dirt track by a speeding pick-up truck with two men inside, and having been warned by Diana Craft in Dallas that I should take care, 'especially of men in open trucks with shotguns in the back', I turn back. I'm looking for the road to another kind of property anyway. An Indian reservation.

It's a long circuitous route. Once you get off the highways, you can easily find yourself on newly-opened roads like the one I mentioned above that quickly disappear into the vast woods that spread out across south eastern Texas. Away from the rapidly expanding cities, you are back among small towns with their populations posted. 2,000-3,000 seems to justify a place being included on my Rand McNally road map. Half the populations of these towns appear to work among the great clutter of neon signs advertising hamburgers and gas and ice cream — Americans, who now have one car between two people, are always on the move — and always hungry, you start to realise.

I flip through the local papers and a blizzard of statistics emerge about America and its habits. Not all of it is good. 500,000 teenagers a year attempt suicide. The rate has doubled since 1960. Only 1 in 100 succeed. Most of these 'successes' are male, though it is a 90% female reaction to the stresses of the teenage years. The rate is rising faster in the West where 'there is too much space and too few people,' the article declares. $1\frac{1}{2}$ million teenagers a year are runaways and approximately half of them are unwanted at home. The teenagers are fleeing from unhappy homes, or sexual abuse or have problems with drug abuse. Americans are living longer, I read next. Although a black man can expect to live 7 years less than his white counterpart (the Indian even less). This is partly explained by the homicide rate which is six times higher among blacks than it is among whites. An angry isolation in blacks finds its outlet against their own kind. There are many black people in Dallas, in fact all of the towns, as they crowd in to find work, doing many of the lower-paid service jobs and powering the economy onwards with their willingness to work hard. All those glittering dreams are built upon this bedrock.

However, instant credit means that those in most kinds of jobs can afford the great gas guzzling cars that temporarily fell from favour during the days of OPEC's effective cartel. The poorer people still believe in the most visible signs of outward success.

Paul Volcker, Chairman of the Reserve Bank, warns that the economy has revived largely due to volatile foreign investment attracted by high interest rates. In 1984, foreign investment provided 23% of all savings. In 1983, it was only 12%. 'There are structural imbalances in the economy that must be cured,' he warns.

Tip O'Neill, Leader of the House of Representatives, is an unreconstructed Democrat. (The newer Democrats are talking about listening to the diverse roots of America's people to find out what they really want, a sure sign that the politicians have lost their way). O'Neill attacks Reagan as 'a kindly old man who is piling up a record deficit.' It has doubled in the five years he has been in control. David Stockman, probable author

An Indian's home on Coushatta Indian Reservation in eastern Texas. With a lake, timberland and a land grant from General Sam Houston, the Indians have a settled life now and are actually assimilating into the Texan population. But they are at home in a way that other Americans still aspire to.

of America's recovery, resigns over the deficit. New statistics point to America's wealth slowly haemorrhaging overseas at the rate of 6% a year. Japan shows a $33 billion surplus in its trade with the USA and talks about taking down some of its trade barriers. Meanwhile, America posts an $88 million trade deficit and, for the first time in 70 years, becomes an overall 'debtor' nation. It is revealed that the banks have lent more than their total assets, in many cases, to the Latin American countries. Where is the Arab oil money finally going to come to rest? Meanwhile, Reagan continues to go for growth as a way out of the vicious circle, but at growth rates never achieved in the past. In his State of the Union message he boasts of the highest year's growth since 1951. Is he going for broke as he simultaneously steps up spending on defence (it is where approximately one dollar in every three of tax revenues is spent — 28%) and cuts domestic programmes to try to balance the budget?

In Texas, it looks as if the strategy is working out. The newspaper classified columns are filled with 'help wanted' ads. From 'Engineers with microprocessor experience, innovative, salary offered $30-50k' to 'telephone canvassers, no selling, $5 an hour, plus commission.'

But back to the Indian reservation. The cars speed by the 3½ mile length of the reservation on the road between Livingstone and Woodville. They pass the only people who feel completely at home on the land. Tall straight trees point up at the crystalline clear stars in the sky. A lake rests under the night. Timber cottages are dotted irregularly about. Dogs wander in the darkness broken only by a few dim lights near the cottages. I go up to a dog that is watching me, wagging its tail, unschooled as it is in being hostile to strangers. It backs off a little, still wagging its tail. 'Children playing,' warns a sign by the road. An Indian woman is sitting in a pick-up truck outside the general store. No alcohol is on sale. Two young Indians come out the store and join the woman. They look like college kids in their baseball jackets and slope easily, lazily along. The woman is fixing her eye make-up in the van. They all smile in amusement as I watch them drive off. I ask the woman in the shop if they still speak their Indian language. Yes, she tells me, they speak both. Are they pure bloods?

'Most, but they're marrying Mexicans and Americans now. There are 400 of us. But there's reservations all over the country, Oklahoma, Arizona, New Mexico, California, Florida.'

The land in Texas was given to them by General Sam Houston. Rising land values, an Indian theatre, camping facilities, tourist attractions, have helped the reservation dwellers to establish a way of living alongside the Texans. In fact, in New Mexico some have become rich, charging entrance fees to drive across their land, allowing the exploitation of minerals. Here in the woods, where it is cold, dark and quiet with the distant sounds of wild animals out there among the trees, a jack rabbit creates a stir scampering among the trunks. It is possible to feel the presence of the vast land, still only 2% of which has been used for urban development. It is a land that has its own rhythms, its own peace... a peace the newer Americans have yet to find. The aggression so necessary in the frontiersmen has yet to mellow in their descendants. At Judge Roy Bean's dance hall the crowd roars along with a Bruce Springsteen video of 'Born in the USA'.

'Forget about California girls,' shouts the DJ, 'haven't we got the best girls here? Texan girls!'

The crowd roars its approval. Bruce Springsteen roars on the video screen.

Mardi Gras in one of the bars on Bourbon St. For once, all the barriers between the races and regions of the country disappear in the rhythms of the song and the singer. A pre-Puritan America emerges, an America that may one day return as it assimilates more of the experience of its southern neighbours, the Spanish descendants.

left
Striptease is another uniquely American invention that relies for its allure on the untouchability of the performer. American women may be militant but they have more to be militant about, a frontier society has little use for the feminine virtues, theirs are more the virtues of a settled life.

Opposite page
One of the elements that goes to make up Mardi Gras is that of the voodoo cults from Haiti, just across the Gulf. Mix this with Spanish, French, Afro-American and British-American influences and you have the recipe for Mardi Gras' magic.

You can hardly miss the parades during the two weeks of Mardi Gras, there's half a dozen every day.

In 1699 the town of New Orleans was founded. In 1985 it remains one of the few centres of a unique American art form — jazz. A little theory before the practice. Jazz was born in a bordello on Bourbon St, part of the Storyville red light district. It reached its early brilliant exposition in the hands of Jelly Roll Morton, who with his syncopated rhythms set the world on fire with desire. Jazz (a slangy black word for sex) has metamorphosed into R&B (Fats Domino, another New Orleans man, was the prime exponent) and then into strident rock'n'roll via Muddy Waters in Chicago and the improvisations of Tamla Motown, The Rolling Stones, The Beatles... the spin-offs are legendary.

But come back to that old sea port in the humid Gulf. The slaves on a Sunday in the early 1800s gather in Congo Square, where with rough-cut drums and calabashes they dance the old rituals they knew (or their forebears knew) in Africa, they are part of the old spirit cults. Mix that influence with the pervasive Creole music of French and Spanish extraction (New Orleans was once a Spanish capital), with the old opera, with the marching songs, with the church music, with the voodoo cults imported via Haiti out of Dahomey, with the blues... and you have the recipe for the genesis of a new kind of music.

'Everyone's got a bit of everything here,' the shoeshine man tells me.

'You tried seafood?.

'Yeah, in Texas,' I tell him. 'When does it get hot here?'

'After about 4 o'clock in the afternoon,' he explains.

New Orleans has a hot time every night. It's the first day of the Mardi Gras parades. There will be 60 parades over the next 2 weeks. Corporate sponsorship of the floats is barred. It's still a local people's celebration, a matter of pride that you contribute. The obvious beneficiaries are the Sheraton, the Marriott, the Royal Sonesta and the Landmark hotels. The last two hotels are situated in Bourbon St (Rue Bourbon) where it all began. In 1917 the Storyville red light district was closed down by the naval military police, in wartime it had become too hot. But by then, the new music had spread out from its birthplace. No wonder a Mormon minister can claim to be able detect drugs, sex, black magic and the bizarre in rock'n'roll. In this street, you realise, those were indeed its original neighbours.

Bourbon Street is still sleazy, but not very, the Americans like to sanitise everything... and Bourbon St of late has become respectable almost, it's firmly placed on the tourist circuit (so are the prices). You pay $3.75 in the Old Opera House for a drink, the same as in that place up the road where, over a drink, you can watch Cindy and Debbie gyrate with tasselled breats to songs like 'It's only physical.... what's love got to do with it?'

'I think when I'm on stage I must give the boys a good time,' says old trooper Cindy, her eyelashes caked thickly black so that they seem to project outwards for several inches.

But if you're new to New Orleans, in Bourbon St, what you have really come for is the music. The band, the singers, have got to be black or creole — like the three girls who keep asking 'Is everyone having a good time?' until they are, until the magic spirit cults of Africa have reasserted their power and everyone, and I mean everyone, is moving to the music, feeling the essential beat... of life, of desire, of the body restored to command over the censorious brain.

Getting ready for the parades, the spectators talk on the streets, frequent the bars, watched by the relaxed New Orleans police force. Prisoners are used to help put up the festival bunting.

'Is it still snowing in Minnesota?' the girl asks as she launches into a jump dance. And she jumps.

The crowds of people sway with their arms, fresh from watching that Mardi Gras parade where the marching songs make you start to move, where the floats glitter with fantastically clad dukes and duchesses. New Orleans had style in the 18th century these costumes remind you.

It's midnight and all the audience — 'Is everyone from out of town?' 'Yeah.' — is singing and shouting along. There are white women with black men, black women with white men, all having a good time.

'What's love got to do with it?' they're asking, these three Creole singers, two are too thin, one is too fat and too short... but on stage they are in control, the music has done its work, we're in a jungle clearing where there is only music and the raw rub of life.

Next morning, the street is restored to its turn-of-the-century essential self. A woman of mixed blood and none too good looking, has a cigarette hanging out of her mouth as she sweeps away the detritus in the gutter. The bar she emerges from is shabby. A man avoids looking into my camera as I turn it on a long line of terraced houses where, empty of people, the gutters choked with rubbish, the old Storyville district comes to faded life again. It's poor, pleasures are few and grabbed quickly, life is short. 'Take what you can,' you hear the houses say. Music to ease the pain, to help you forget? Or an assertion of life triumphant, of life overcoming the odds and succeeding in celebration?

It is Sunday. New Orleans is quiet. There are no slaves on Congo Square dancing those almost forgotten African rituals. Now it's called Louis Armstrong Park. On the radio they are arguing the case for integrating the predominantly black colleges. One of the college principals counsels that the predominant race in the integrated schools is the white race, they edit the college newspaper, take up the leadership positions.

'Should we integrate our black churches?' he rhetorically asks.

But that music in Bourbon St is the great grandchild of a black Africa that believed, and it is still promulgating its beliefs to us today. The message is garbled but the rhythm is clear. It is giving the white man back his body, one day he won't (and she won't) throw it away through neglect.

'I tour. Been here 7 weeks,' says Debbie. 'Do it in Florida, Nevada, Massachusetts, California.'

Her face is sincere, her body is already overweight and over-indulged. Let the good times roll. They haven't yet.

# THE GULF

The addiction of travelling is being free as the wind. The Gulf of Mexico at this moment is throwing a howling rain storm at me, so that the drops of water richochet off my — fortunately — thick jacket. Among the backwaters back from north Lido beach (just off the main part of Sarasota) an egret was the only other creature out in the storm. It took off at my approach, as wild as the landscape. A few hardy windsurfers were catapulting up and down on the frothing waves but now the winds have become too strong for them, you bend almost double fighting your way back up the beach. On a good day, the 'naturists' take over the beach, it is suitably discreet with trees marching up to the fine white sand of the shoreline, but there is no sign of them today. That would be foolhardy. The weatherman called for 74 degrees on the radio as I passed close to Orlando on the way down, but the Sarasota forecast is not so hopeful with tomorrow predicted to be 'not even reaching the 60s'.

A pity. It was the lure of the heat which persuaded me to drive the 500 miles from New Orleans in one long marathon. Through the bayous of Louisiana, and the long straight empty roads of the Florida panhandle. On turning south, after the long drive east, in the first large town — Tallahassee — you sense the tropic nature of the state, the many Latin-looking people, the humidity in the air, the sense that General Winter does not wreak his devastations so far south. But this storm on the beach has an intensity to it, even without the northern chill. The Gulf is moody. All night long the palms will be bending in the storm as it lashes the coast. I reflect on that road sign I passed leaving New Orleans — 'Hurricane Evacuation Route'.

Long distances are an inescapable and ultimately hypnotic feature of American travel. On the empty road at night you see nothing but the cats eyes leading you onwards, the land is sensed rather than seen but its power is all the more real for that. It is unknown and unpredictable. The car is invaded by a rotten smell. I wind down the car window.

'That's a pulp mill, not me,' laughs Jimmy Smoey, my hitchiker guide to Florida. He'd reached as far as Mobile in Alabama after two and half days on the road from Oklahoma City where he'd been to see his sister. Seems he once lived there, had a full-blood Indian bride. They had 6 kids between them, he two, she four. She qualified for a house at a rental of $25, being a full-blood, but Jimmy only found this out when he had built his own. Then his business failed, like the marriage. Now at age 42, he is married to a woman of 62, who hands him money when he's short. 'She's really good to me,' he explains.

He works as a nurse for four or five hours a day and earns $250 a week. He looks after those who have 'old people's disease — the brain just steadily deteriorates, nothing they can do about it. At the end they just can't control their functions, they crap themselves, pee at the table.'

'There's a lot of land here,' I say in the Florida panhandle.

'I hope it never gets built up,' he replies.

We stop at a roadstop café in the midst of the emptiness of the panhandle, but here at least, two roads intersect. Once inside, Nick the Greek bashes our ears as we admire the 'wild horses and log cabin' pictures on the walls of the log cabin style café-diner.

Nick asks Jimmy if he knows anyone who might want to buy the place. 'It's too big for me,' he says, 'needs someone with a large family. There's only four of us, I had no education, but I tell you there'll always be 8 million, 12 million unemployed unless there's a war. That's the only time there's full employment. I don't believe Reagan, there won't be no social security

Previous page 82-83

Vast orange groves dominate the centre of Florida. In 1985 the crop was subjected to the hammer blows of frosts in January, drought in June and hurricanes in August/September. The Fruit Board operates strict quality control to ensure that your Florida orange juice is the finest Suspect crops are not permitted to be picked.

Previous page 84-85

North Lido Beach, Sarasota, is a haven of natural tranquility where no building is permitted. Naturists and birds frequent its shores.

Previous page 86-87

The backwaters off Lido Beach harbour an astonishing amount of wildlife, which is surprising considering the rapid development of Satasota, fuelled by migrating retirees. The obituary columns are full of stories of people who lived most of their lives in the North, then came South to die.

The Florida high season gets under way at the end of January and lasts through until May. But the Gulf is an unpredictable sea, fierce storms blow in suddenly and dramatically bend back the palms and shoreline vegetation. Hurricane Elena, for example, resulted in hundreds of thousands evacuating their homes during the hurricane alert.

cuts, not even through the back door.'

Jimmy Smoey tells me about the Indians he knew in Oklahoma.

'They'd get a social security check for $500, take it down the bar, give it the barman and just keep drinking. Two or three days later the barman would say "It's gone". They're so out of their brain they don't know. Just can't take alcohol, the Indians.'

The sea is churning up past the car on the shoreline in Sarasota. Time to check into a motel, as the front of the car is battered by a wave that shakes the suspension. The rate is merely $85 a day for the 2 double-bedded room with kitchen and bathroom off. When I say I'll look elsewhere the owner, kitted out in a cowboy-style string tie, reduces the rate to the off-peak $65.

'Don't tell no-one else,' he requests, 'there's people here paying the full peak rate. The weather's not good is it?'

'No, and tomorrow it's forecast to be colder.'

Sunset is sunny, almost balmy. The averge temperature in Sarasota, just south of St Petersburg on Tampa Bay, is 72 degrees; 62 degrees in winter, 82 degrees in summer. The car registrations I see seem to be entirely from the northern states — Ohio, Illinois, Minnesota... a check on the weather map reveals that these states are in the grip of below-freezing-point temperatures. Quite exceptionally, the arctic blasts penetrated even halfway down the Florida peninsula at the end of January killing much of the citrus crop.

'The whole center is one long orange grove,' Jimmy had explained.

Sarasota is the third fastest growing metropolitan area in the nation, as people and businesses relocate to the sunbelt. The city is the second richest in what is a very rich state. There is no local tax — an added attraction to the new rich–the retired. They are to be found in great congregations all over Florida, 'cities of the living dead,' says Jimmy.

'My father has an Army pension, a Federal pension, a special pension because he spent over 20 years overseas with the Army. He's got so much that he doesn't know what to do with it. He's had four coronary by-pass operations, bought a Pontiac, sold it after 6 weeks because he didn't like it, and for a $4,000 loss.'

Yachts bob in the marina, big new cars sit beside them. The pristinely clean shops are full of 'tasteful' art and clothes. Sarasota's residents talk about the peaceful calm of the place.

'I can be a beach bum here and have a nice home,' says one celebrity in the local giveaway magazine for intending residents.

Florida — and Sarasota — has been a place of boom and bust before in its short history. The first settlers hereabouts date from the 1840s. Before that it was a pirate haven. Plantation owners using slave labour made the first fortunes. Then there were the great land booms and busts of the 1930s. I notice a local estate agent is fighting 5 mortgage foreclosures in the local courts, he owes a total of $½ million. You realise that any place has an unspoken but sensed history, always liable to reassert itself, even if in different form.

# SARASOTA

No one knows the derivation of the name Sarasota. The area was once inhabited by Indians, and was known to the Spanish from the mid-1500s. The subtropical temperatures make it a little like Spain in feel, as do the numerous palms and the Spanish style buildings. The old Florida, agricultural and cut off on the peninsula from the far-off industrial north, has changed into a place like Australia with all the signs of rapid urban sprawl around the cities.

Last year, 1 in 25,000 of the inhabitants of Sarasota was murdered. A probable contract killing of a New Yorker thought to have gangster connections. It remains unsolved. The murder of an estate developer who had made many enemies, so many it seems that the police have again been unable to detect his murderer. And the bizarre murder of a man, who police believe, hired someone to rough up his wife. The thug beat up the wrong woman. In the ensuing argument with his paymaster, the thug shot him dead and escaped. Identity of murderer still unknown.

Sarasota wants to become smart. At the Magic Moment Club on Midnight Pass Road in Siesta Key they have David Clayton Thomas on the bill (a key is one of the small islands off the coast in Sarasota Bay and further down the coast — hence the famous and fabled Key West, home for Hemingway, one of the last of the great chain of islands that reach out from the tip of Florida towards Cuba just 90 miles away). David Clayton Thomas former lead singer with Blood, Sweat and Tears, is a big draw. 'We've had Chubby Checker, Brenda Lee, lots of people who had a hit about five years ago,' the barmaid explains.

'So it's a bit like Las Vegas?'

'No, they have people like Dean Martin there,' she patiently continues.

'This is for the younger generation and the middle-aged, not...'

'Geriatrics?'

'Right.'

The audience reverentially gather for the show, dressed in expensive but casual clothes. A man who looks like the displayed photograph of David Clayton Thomas approaches the bar on the other side of the room. He has a wide-open brightly coloured shirt, long hair although he's balding on top, a paunch, and wears jeans together with western boots. To complete the outfit he has a gold chain around his neck. As the show begins I realise he is a roady. Into view comes David Clayton Thomas. He wears a light coloured jacket, underneath an open-necked shirt, jeans, western boots... his hair, though long, is balding, he has a small paunch. He only comes alive singing the old hits, the audience cheers as he goes into his favourite number.

'This song's one I always close with, it's been very good to me over the last 15 years, and for the next 15 I hope. Hope it's very good for you... I thought I was in love before, but when you walked through that door...'

The show closes. Two girls from the front seats are ushered backstage to meet the band.

America has closed its welcoming embrace over even the dissident 60s generation, but then they achieved success, that is the final determinant.

The only part of the keys in Sarasota Bay that is underdeveloped is north Lido Beach. The southern part of the beach is dotted with everything from a Holiday Inn to a Sheraton charging $90 a room a night. The peak season rates begin in February and last through to May. The fleeing Northerners are prepared to pay.

Previous page

British racing driver, John Watson, climbs out of his Camarro at the pits during practice for the Daytona Speedway 500. Speeds reach in excess of 200mph.

Former Blood, Sweat and Tears lead singer, David Clayton Thomas, sings his greatest hits to a predominantly 30-40 year-old audience at the Magic Moment nightclub. The old 'youth' culture is rapidly becoming the new establishment.

Back on north Lido Beach only the often blown-down trees are in permanent residence. And streams. And birds. I come upon a hawk sitting on a branch just back from the shore. He allows me to come up really close for a picture, stares impassively ahead. In the sea a few surfers are trying out the breakers whipped up by the blustering wind. There is no-one else around. It is a snippet of the Florida visitors expect to find, but the influx of people means that only the national parks are undeveloped now.

The young and old are in evidence. There are no families at this time of year, no children. The old — beside dying in large numbers — frequent the tidy restaurants and patronise the expensive boutiques. The young gather at the clubs, modern like all the town. Winter is too close for the laziness of summer to be upon the people. It seems tornedoes touched down in Mobile, Alabama and Pensacola, Florida during the night of the storm. The weatherman says the weather will become less predictable, temperatures will fall to the mid 30s overnight and only reach 60 again tomorrow.

Back at the Magic Moment, David Clayton Thomas is doing the second show of the evening. There's a buzz coming from the speakers. He storms off-stage asking if the management has bought the equipment in K-Mart. He returns.

'We've traced the cause of the trouble, fluctuating electricity supply. Guess we won't be able to sing any ballads.'

There's a cry of disappointment from the audience.

'Sometimes in winter, forgotten memories come drifting through the trees and call your name...' a flute plays.

'Here's a Muddy Waters song, one of my great influences...' afterwards a flute plays the intro to Sometime in Winter again and a look of nostalgia for the good times comes over the predominantly 30ish audience as the singer sings from some private haunted world where that song came from, it has powered him into a way of life, given him a following... the flute intro stops and a rock 'n' roll number takes over, he resumes his Las Vegas style of happy-go-lucky minstrel having momentarily let the mask drop. Yet it was the depth of those early songs, their sweet doubt, which gave him his appeal. Appearances to the contrary, the lacquered and layered audience, glittering in their casual finery, came for a questioning of the human condition, not, after all, to forget. Now there is only the escape of glamour...

'And when I'm dead, and when I'm gone, there'll be one more child to carry on, to carry on.'

'Ladies and gentlemen, David Clayton Thomas, former lead singer with Blood, Sweat and Tears.'

The show must go on.

'Please stand back from the fence, this may be a practice, but they are race cars,' says the racetrack commentator as four cars — seemingly linked together — roar down the outside of the straight at well over 200mph.

The cars are Camarros, all brought up to the same standard so that it is 'simply a test of the driver's skill'. One of the ways that the drivers can gain an advantage, is to position themselves so closely behind the car in front that they are dragged along in the partial vacuum created by the slipstream and can then shoot out with a burst of acceleration at the approach of a bend. Daytona Speedway's bends are massively banked so that the hurtling speeds attained on the straights are barely diminished if the driver can withstand the painful 'g' forces the turns entail.

I talk my way into the pits. There's John Watson, British champion, here for the Daytona 500 when 12 international drivers will pit themselves against each other two days hence. Today is first day of practice. Watson, aquiline featured, dressed in immaculate soft clothing, climbs out of his Camarro, safety helmet as all-embracing as a space helmet. His clothing and helmet are peppered with the names of his sponsors and among them is a Union Jack. He begins to talk to one of the American drivers. Both look calm, thoughtful, in icy control of themselves. Watson screws up his face as he talks about moving out of the slipstream of the car in front and being buffeted by the 200mph blast of the air. The cars jet past.... whoooom..... physically knocking you aside with the force of the displaced air, deafening you with the engine roar that sounds like a low flying plane. They climb up the bank of the bend and disappear from sight.

Motels all along Daytona Beach welcome race fans here for the big carnival. Topless go-go dancers are advertised outside the bars with their own form of welcome. At the silky white beach, with a glow of sunset on the sky, cars drive along in a rite of farewell to the sun, the beach stretches for miles in a vast flat expanse becoming progressively tinged by the colours of the sky. A young man on a bike engages a girl seated in a car in animated conversation. There is no litter to be seen, a few sea birds dot the purple colour sky. So perfect a beach has inevitably been built-up all along its length, mile after mile. You have to head south as far as Cape Canaveral to find untouched shoreline on the densely populated eastern side of Florida where the motels vie for custom with an awesome politeness. But to see that parade of cars on the beach at sunset is to find a beauty in the distant lights of the motels against the backdrop of a mighty ocean.

Apart from the races, there's another attraction in this part of the world for the winter vacationers. Disney World, situated some 80 miles inland in a park as big as Manhattan Island, the center of New York City. This stunning fact is given to me by the courtesy train attendant as we ferry between the Pluto aisle of the car park and the entrance to the Magic Kingdom. Across the shining blue lake a fairy castle rises up that is reached by a Mississippi paddle boat. The captain waves in recognition of another soul arriving to meet his vision of heaven. The girl in the stall selling Donald Duck and Goofy souvenirs has a larger-than-life personality. She seems to squeak as she be-

Daytona Beach is crisp white sand for mile after mile. One of the more extraordinary sights is to see the cars driving along the beach in a motorised version of the evening stroll.

Disney World near Orlando, Florida attracts millions of visitors each year who are greeted by the attendants in a manner that previously only happened in Walt Disney movies. If only that was how life really was. Or perhaps it is. Perhaps that was Disney's hold on us all.

comes animated like a cartoon character. She is also exceptionally nice and wholesome — she's Miss Rabbity, and very very pretty. There are more adults in view than kids... but then they have more of a need to believe in goodness. A couple of 6-year-olds already think it's going to be a 'great day' as they descend on the entrance turnstiles with their parents in tow. There's a lot of innate goodness in America, the attendants are all exceptionally nice, you expect them to muse, 'Well, why can't everyday be like Christmas?' You know that somewhere, sometime, it was and is. That's the rub.

Further up the coast is an older America, St Augustine, the oldest city in America in fact. In the town square is a heavily restored old market place known as the Slave Market, which for the majority of its life is what it was. People have been doing business here since 1598, ruled first by the Spaniards, briefly the English, finally the Americans. By the seafront is a pub with some of the atmosphere of days gone by, but not without trace. The Tradewinds Lounge. A very long-haired band is playing, many bearded, big, relaxed characters sit around, descendants of those who fought on the warm waters here for possession of the land and its wealth. Descendants of slave owners and overseers.

Today, they still have a rough belief in themselves, and are not committed to the latter-day angst that has beset their neighbours far to the north — perhaps because they have less of the German race's blood in their veins. The lineage of the majority of Americans is divided almost equally between British, Irish and German ancestry — it forms the background of some 150 of the 230 millions in America today. But the later-arriving Germans settled in the North.

# MARCHING THROUGH GEORGIA

It is a bright sunny day in north Florida. Valentine's Day. The waitress has a heart in lipstick on her cheek but is not outwardly cheerful. The road northwards is quiet, many of the cars have an Ohio, Indiana or Michigan destination — some 1,700 miles to the north. In these states there are heavy falls of snow that have cut off towns, bus drivers are refusing to take their vehicles out. The snow hit northern Georgia too, especially in the mountains but down south it simply gradually gets colder and cloudy. The Suwannee meanders lazily promising the sloth of summer. A perfectly white cat sits at the side of the road. It is the heart of the old Confederacy. Not too much of its legacy is left unless you include the extraordinary interregnum of the Carter presidency when a southern earnest morality briefly held sway at the White House. After the excesses of Vietnam and Watergate the whole nation became as disenchanted with Federal government as the South has always been in living memory.

The old South... there are road signs pointing to plantation houses... where the old southern aristocracy amassed a staggering wealth from a single crop... King Cotton... and the free labour supplied by the slaves. Today, the South East is once again the fastest growing area of the USA, the new fortunes founded on the post-industrial technologies, IBM has some of its major offices here... as does the oil industry... Ted Carter with his Cable Network News... Coca Cola with its HQ in Georgia.

'It's that Federal Government,' moans the man in the general store in Macon. The old bitterness remains... especially in Georgia. Here you can see examples of pre-bellum architecture that survived General Sherman's notorious march to the sea when he cut a 60-mile swath of destruction and misery on his journey from Atlanta. That, and subsequent plunder, reduced the South to abject second-class economic status for over 100 years. It took a peanut farmer to arise and apply the balm of reconciliation to a nation once again split in two by Vietnam.

But you could argue that Reagan, too, is a continuation of the celebration of old American values — except that his come from a later period. That of the 19th century immigrants who opened up the mid-West, who farmed the plains and saw wealth grow out of the soil in return for hard effort. They were part of the great push westwards that came to a stop in California, where Reagan like millions before him was part of the enactment of the American dream in those beautiful lands beyond the Rocky Mountains.

This final push to the sea took place in the aftermath of the Civil War, the years 1860-1890 were the source of all those western stories and heroes which Hollywood commemorated. It was the most lawless of times, when personal freedom (the rallying cry of the war for both sides) saw out its most extravagant interpretations. It led to the dispossession of the red man, as forts preceded settlers who grabbed the land. To them the land lay undeveloped.

Standing high above a pass which leads on through Colorado to Arizona, to California and finally the sea. My Indian guide looks down with me. We see the wagon trains below pouring into the great empty spaces of America. All roads for nearly a century have been leading to this promised land of California, the wealthiest state in the nation.

Opposite page

The Suwannee lazily drifts through the borders of Georgia and Florida, the steam boats have come and gone but that ol' man river he just keeps rolling, he just keeps rolling along.

A Louisiana bayou provides a perfect outlet for the numerous sportsmen who fish and hunt along its winding length.

# I LEFT MY HEART IN SAN FRANCISCO

The two fastest growing states in the USA are California and Texas. The most celebrated city — in songs at least — is San Francisco. It is a visual experience. Imagine travelling the 8 miles of bridge spanning San Francisco Bay as you journey from Oakland to the city itself after Interstate Highway 80 comes to journey's end nearly 3,000 miles from New York City.

The night time city rears up on the steep hills. Behind the buildings, shot through with lights, is a wealth of grey-white clouds caught in the beams of an early rising moon. The city is breathtaking. And does not disappoint on entering, either. Here is the Wells Fargo Bank, founded in 1852, here are many buildings built (or rebuilt after the 1906 earthquake) in the late 19th-century colonial style. The city has been carefully preserved from the worst excesses of modern development. Pastel shaded houses climb the hills in terraces, the hills are so steep that road signs urge car parkers to engage gear and handbrake, and turn the front wheels into the kerb. To be driving down these hills is definitely an experience, similar to plunging down a ski run with some initial trepidation to be followed by the thrill of the descent.

I am talking to one of most reliable sources of information about any city — a shoeshine man. David Hamilton shines the shoes for a dollar. (I tip him for his info). 'I figured the time to do some travelling was while I was still young enough. How old are you? 39, like me?'
I add a year, it should be two.
'It never snows here. Not like Chicago, where I come from. I'm moving on to Texas soon. Then up to New York. What do you think of Reagan?'
I'm non-commital.
'Yeah, I agree with him cutting down the welfare, look at me, I don't get nothing from my taxes, I'm a working man. (This could all be for my benefit, agreeing with the customer's view of life). Some people say he's anti-black people. I don't. He just wants to cut taxes. I'm not political now though, not like in 68. I was at the protests in Chicago — at the Democrat Convention. My mama stopped me going to Vietnam. She got in touch with the preacher, why did I wanna go killing babies? They don't treat those vets no good. It was a dirty war. I wanted nothing of it. Yeah, the protests were worth it.'

Whether David Hamilton has been accepted back by that society is debatable, but he's learnt the value of protest, he's learnt his rights, that is a lesson that will come in handy should it ever be needed. Now's he following another American tradition, freedom, moving on down the line, it was how California was founded, the movement goes on.

Some of the first people to reach California were the Chinese. For on the other side of the great ocean, Asia begins, and it looms large in the settled Californian's mentality. Behind him mountains, ahead of him sea, he sees himself as an island between the West and the East, and a possible bridge. Part of the Pacific Region which the 21st century will push forward. Clouds drift off the moody Pacific, seeming to be tunnelled into the San Francisco Bay area. It's usually a few degrees cooler here than even in the neighbouring counties — where the expansion of the city is now taking place up to 50 miles away.

Previous page

USS Pampanito, the last surviving submarine from World War II at anchor on Pier 45 in San Francisco Bay. Over 1.5 million GI's passed through the harbour on their way to the Pacific war. Many settled in California on their return. In the background is the former Federal penitentiary of Alcatraz. There are guided tours of both vessel and island.

Outside the Pacific Missile Test Center is an early Polaris nuclear missile. Californians have little of the East Coast's diffidence about possessing such awesome naked power. 1 in 8 of them work for the military. America and Russia between them possess warheads with the destructive power of 50,000 Hiroshima bombs.

There's a trial on in town. It happened far out at sea in the Pacific, on remote Palmyra Atoll, some 500 miles north of the equator, and below Hawaii. In August 1974, a San Diego couple were murdered on the atoll and it was only in 1981 that the woman's bleached bones were discovered hidden in a half-buried casket on the island. Her husband's body has never been found. Another couple who had arrived at the atoll on a leaking boat are accused of the murder.

But at the same time as the Californians have reached out into the Pacific, the Chinese have come in from the great Pacific Basin. In the mid-1800s the rich were sending their laundry on the astonishingly quick clipper ships to China. The laundrymen rightly saw the opportunity to return with the washing to these prosperous customers. The result is China-town, the largest Chinese settlement outside Asia. Sandwiched in among sex shows offering wall-to-wall sex and male strippers, there are some fine eating houses. The Golden Dragon is so dark that you can hardly see. The tables are close together, the hostesses wear long slit-to-the-thigh satin dresses as they guide you to your seat rather like a cinema usherette. The sea food in particular is superb — and in San Franciso you should not pass up the opportunity.

Another area of town packed with eating houses is Fisherman's Wharf, at the foot of the hills that make up the town, reached by cable car, where there are any number of fine restaurants offering views across the bay to the former penitentiary of Alcatraz. Fisherman's Wharf is thronged with a restless tide of tourists, all in good humour and perpetually distracted by the sights and sounds of street buskers, and shops offering such intriguing wares as authentic 19th-century photographs where girls in saloon-bar dresses drape themselves around you. It does give a quintessential glimpse of the true San Francisco, a hell-raising town in its day if ever there was one.

Two girls from Pittsburgh — 'the worst city in America' — get a busker, spending his day's takings at the bar, to take their photograph.

The night sky is lit by a strange light in the atmosphere. Next morning the North American Defence Command in Colorado Springs, Colorado, states that there is no cause for concern. It was aware 'of a test launch activity along the West Coast.' It seems a missile was being tested 300 miles off the San Franciso coast along a firing range which extends south to 300 miles off the coast at San Diego, a distance of some 600 miles. The 'fairly routine firing' was simply to test 'the missile system effectiveness of a ballistic missile submarine,' states Don Levis, spokesman for the Navy's Pacific Missile Test Center on the Ventura County coast.

One in eight Californians works for the defence industries. There is no great sense of unease, simply curiosity. The huge build-up in American defence forces continues to underwrite the richest state in the nation's prosperity.

# NO, SAN FRANCISCO PEOPLE ARE NOT BORING

The great annual American Booksellers Association book fair is drawing to a close. Books on every subject from 'reading eyes' to glossy fantasies of an ever more escapist nature have been bought and sold. (It seems there are ways of determining from eye colour whether a person is a spring, summer, autumn, or winter kind of person with a consequent difference in what colours they should wear and in what their character is like.) Now the participants get down to the serious business of enjoying themselves. They know that as long as the economy stays good the great American public will continue to buy their offerings in dizzying numbers.

First, there is a party at City Lights bookshop. These publishers and booksellers of avant garde poetry from the 50s, 60s and early 70s live in a rather battered bookshop up the hill from the Bank of America's futuristic pyramid skyscraper in Columbus Avenue. Lawrence Ferlinghetti plays host to the assorted publishers and literary groupies who have spilled out onto the sidewalk as they drink an innocuous-tasting but highly effective cocktail containing champagne and brandy. As the alcohol permeates bloodstreams, the talk flows copiously. 'We're hoping to have Andrei Voznesensky here tomorrow,' Lawrence Ferlinghetti tells me 'but he's booked on United.' (United pilots are on strike and the company is busily recruiting new pilots and looks set for the long haul.) I tell Ferlinghetti I met him in Australia in 1972.
'Oh yes, I was with Alan (Ginsberg).'

Now he looks much older (he has a white beard) and also less intense. His latest book is about a visit to Nicaragua. Ferlinghetti describes himself as a libertarian with anarchist leanings. Reagan has started to refer to the Marxist-Leninist Government as Communists, and to the 'contras' as freedom fighters. You sense a small country about to be overtaken by the enormous forces of the 'Great Game' — or so 19th century British statesmen referred to their shadow boxing with the Russian Empire on the fringes of the Raj in India. There is little of the old Ferlinghetti poetry in the shop. He has a book of his illustrations on the theme of the nude, on display. The eyes are still angelically blue... has the vision become narrowed down to political terminology? An air of dissoluteness hangs over the muddy brown colours of the bookshop — displaying volumes by Henry Miller, Gary Snyder, Alan Ginsberg, Bukowsky and William Burroughs... it is the beat generation nearly 30 years on. The faces at the party all tell a story, or two. Publisher John Calder from London. He now divides his time between Britain and America. He very painstakingly reviewed the author's first precocious novel. But in spite of his avant garde reputation, gained from publishing Last Exit to Brooklyn he is grey-suited, balding and guarded like all the big publishers. John Calder also published much of Henry Miller, which raises his claims to literary discernment. His erstwhile partner Marion Boyars, is also here. But they don't speak. Miller's face looks strongly out from a bookjacket, perhaps he found restoration at Big Sur down the coast, he moved on, those at this party have become stranded at the high tide mark of a current that has moved elsewhere.

Previous page
Poet Lawrence Ferlinghetti and friend at a literary reception in San Francisco's City Lights bookshop on Columbus. It was once the center of a whole literary movement during the time of the 'beat' poets.

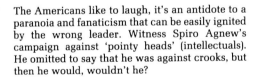

The energy this night, this year, this decade is more likely to be found at Bookpeople's and Publishers Group West's party. Both these companies, based in San Francisco, are distributors for the burgeoning number of small publishers that have taken up the literary running in America over the last 10 years. Ferlinghetti's press, New Directions, was an early precursor of this latter-day explosion.. but now there are many more self-help and self-improvement manuals, less rooted in the literary culture, more part of a new philosophy. What the beats pulled down left room for the new philosophies to grow.

There are four storeys in the Gift Centre where the ball is held. I invite my old boss, Jim Mercer, along. I explain that it may be a rather stuffy affair.

'No,' he says, 'San Francisco people are never boring.'

He is right. It's a thronged, crowded, bustling concert/dance/party where a band of seven fronted by four girls doing a white Tamla Motown act rhythmically bop and shake and move their arms in time, as they urge the people to dance, dance, dance. A tide of arms rise back and forth in perfect unison as though swept by tidal gusts.

Here's Theresa from upstate New York on her last night in town. She's moving along to the frantic beat, the inhibitions of even 20 years ago don't inhabit her generation's frames. Here's Joan, also on her last night in town, she works, I think she says above the din, for The American Publisher, she puts her bag down on the floor.

'It's got all my worldly goods,' she smiles.

Dazzling light comes out of her eyes. She is getting down, literally, she vibrates slowly towards the floor. One of the fair books had an explanation. 'Light is transmitted from the deepest levels of a person, it can be blocked by fears acquired in childhood, but unobstructed it emanates out and bathes the world, finding communion on an unspoken deep level.'

Later, looking down on the multi-coloured, all-dancing mass of bodies moving to the beat, Joan marvels at the beauty of it all. It is some party.

The Americans like to laugh, it's an antidote to a paranoia and fanaticism that can be easily ignited by the wrong leader. Witness Spiro Agnew's campaign against 'pointy heads' (intellectuals). He omitted to say that he was against crooks, but then he would, wouldn't he?

When John Steinbeck wrote Cannery Row, the fishing industry on Monterey Peninsula was the main source of income for the area's inhabitants. No longer. A new aquarium has opened up on Cannery Row generating a lot of money in its wake. Opened in November 84, it was expected to attract 400,000 visitors a year to this quiet rural spot where ice plants form a temporary blaze of luscious colour for six weeks in the late spring. Small bijou houses line the Pacific Ocean but the visitors are making their mark. In 8 months over 1,000,000 have poured in. Good fortune for suddenly upgraded establishments like Alisa's which was once a house of ill-repute and featured in a Steinbeck novel.

The aquarium has cutaway tanks showing you otters diving below water, and a stunning collection of plants and intertidal life. None more so than the lobsters that have made their home on the foundations of the building where it juts out into the Pacific.

My orientation on Monterey comes from two informants. Ruby Grace is the first. She is Marketing Manager for Angel Press — a small 'new age' publisher. 'In God we trust,' she says, while discussing the buying of lists of people into the 'new age' way of thinking.

'Basically, they're on the coasts, New England, Pennsylvannia, Florida, California, some in Texas too,' she adds. Their shop is very Spanish in style, like much of the town (until about 120 years ago, Monterey was the capital of the then Spanish province of California). The books they display range from Sexual Secrets (recommended reading) to Aurobindo's writings published by the Self Realisation Fellowship based near Los Angeles. Angel Press also print and bind their books on the premises, in spite of an 8-month hiatus when they had to wait for the right electrical transformer to be installed. Ruby's just back from an inland camping trip.

'It's much better than here on the coast,' she claims enthusiastically.

Back outside the quiet whitewashed building, I take in the view from the Outrigger over a Mai Tai cocktail. The ocean looks beautiful. A couple wander out after finishing their cocktails.

'She'll do anything you want her to do,' says the waitress.
The woman, in her 40s, giggles. It's vacation time.

I have an address and phone number given me back in England. I ring. Ask for Karen.
'Yes, this is Karen,' a girlish voice answers.
But she's not the Karen I was given the name of.
'Oh, I know Jana too,' she says encouragingly, 'come on round.'
Karen lives in a house with 'Welcome Friends' emblazoned above a pair of white doves in the doorway. I bang on the door, which is in any case open.
Karen comes to the door. She's a woman of about 35 I guess, not so girlish after all. She offers me a drink. We're soon deep in conversation.
'Everyone comes from somewhere else in California,' she says quickly enough after explaining that she came from Austria when she was eight years old. Her father is English, her mother German, they live in Europe. Even though she has spent some time in Germany, she is unrepentant in her choice of country to reside in.

The mountains come down to the sea all along the Big Sur coastline. Orson Welles built his honeymoon home for Rita Hayworth here. It's called Nepenthe's. Henry Miller lived in Big Sur for 15 years and loved its wilderness.

Previous page

Monterey Peninsula, scene of John Steinbeck's *Cannery Row* novel. For six weeks the ice plants along the shore add a dramatic intensity to the already rich colours of the bay.

Look at the photograph closely and you'll see the overturned chassis of a Mercedes which crashed over the cliff the night before. It's center picture where the burnt vegetation begins. There are a lot of accidents on the Big Sur coast road.

'It's easier here,' she says.

Her 19-year-old daughter rings.

'She lives with her boyfriend,' her mother declares warmly, 'but she rings me a dozen times a week, I must have done something right bringing her up.'

Karen works as a technician in a hospital specialising in cardiac trouble. I comment about the steadiness of the work.

'It was alright until about three years ago, now they're economising, sometimes I'm put on call and half pay, but it's worse for the nurses, there aren't many trained people like me. I think being administrator of a hospital now has to be one of the worst jobs. Working out how soon they can send people back home.'

'But the doctors do very well,' I suggest to her.

'Sure but I wouldn't like their workload. They really work.'

I eventually learn that Karen is separated from her photographer husband. John arrives. He works in Defence, studying Russian. I get up to go, having been regaled with tales of Big Sur where 'the mountain people come into the bars, River Inn, for instance and Nepenthe's (a honeymoon nest for Orson Welles), I go there a lot, just to look at the people, they're such an interesting bunch.'

Later that night I'm in the bar, admiring the bargirl's fine necklace, a face of Indian-style inscrutability looks at me.

'There's a lot of artists up here,' she says by way of reply.

Big Sur was written up by Henry Miller, who extolled its rugged beaty at some length. The coast road winds in and out of the mountains that reach right down to the sea. You feel in the River Inn that you are in the mountains. The locals are cracking jokes, having a lot of fun.

'You need a car to get anywhere in California,' a waitress says, 'I knew a woman who bought a Mercedes just to get to the bathroom.'

Out on the coast road again and down to Pfeiffer's Beach, to be found off to the right just before a bridge some three miles past River Inn. For three miles the road twists and turns, getting narrower as it goes. A bird, accompanied by a dozen young, scurries across the road at this unusual disturbance from the outside world. A man is stroking two horses in a field. The road peters out just before the beach, which is windswept and dominated by great rocks against which the sea crashes. It needs to be pretty hot before you can spend time here.

The Pacific winds (and currents) come down from the North, from the coasts of Oregon and Washington and Canada. It gives a coolness to the shore, in spring and early summer. Especially as the far hotter interior draws off great shrouds of mist that don't clear till midday.

Along the spectacular coast road again. We stop at a spot where firemen with their water wagon are putting out some smouldering vegetation. It's the aftermath of a crash that happened the previous night. The fireman explains.

'He was driving along at up to a 100, forced a couple of people off the road, hit that bank there, it flipped him over and down the cliff.'

The upturned car is to be seen some 150 feet down the precipitous side of the cliff, tangled in the undergrowth.

'What happened to him?'

'The driver? He's all burnt up.'

'Dead?'

'Yeah dead, now you drive carefully.'

Eventually on the drive south, the fog-shrouded spurs of Big Sur's mountains dropping precipitously into the sea give way to a more green land. Along route 101 you turn off for Alvia Beach just after San Luis Obispo. Two miles down the road, you head off right by the golf course along a track marked 'No through road' to the left of some oil storage tanks. The other side of the bluff, you find a car park and then descend to Pirate's Cove along a steeply dropping track that takes you to the beach lined for its entire length by 100-foot high cliffs. Out in the cool Pacific, seals fight and grunt as they battle for prime basking places on the rocks that protrude above the sea at low tide.

It's very quiet here, given over to naturists. A little self-consciously, with none of that European nonchalence, the two dozen or so people are scattered along the 300-foot beach in small groups. Some of the girls wear their bikini bottoms, here's one playing with her dog, she has tiny breasts with no filling of flesh in the upper hemispheres. Her dog enthusiastically pursues the sticks she is throwing into the sea. The only other interruption is when the dog stops momentarily to cock its ears as it hears the seals grunting at each other again, there is a brief fracas as a third seal tries to dislodge the two who are sunbathing on the rock. This is only big enough for two, the third interloper obstinately establishes a place for itself and one of the original two eventually leaves. *Force majeure.*

Quiet returns to the cove. The only woman who passes muster when disrobed, puts on her bikini bottom to go for a paddle along the sea shore. An hour later, she is feeling braver and now prances in the sea with her boyfriend, nakedly white, red haired and exuberant. They make a fine happy young couple, the girl more boisterous than the man who, you suspect, is happy to let the world admire from far his heart's desire.

In the sheltered cove it's impossible to take the sunseekers by sudden surprise. 100 feet up on the cliff tops, two men throw down packs for their friends below. They crash down the cliff face, raising a minor dust storm. The men are perched precariously on their car's roof which is parked right at the cliff edge. Peace again returns to the cove — the seals grunt again. People drift off to begin the long ascent up the powdery dusty path.

Back on the road heading south, to Santa Barbara; you have to take exposure to the sun in brief stages because of the fierce sun rays of southern California. Life in the open air, heady as it is, needs to be approached gradually. Most skin cancers are caused by sudden prolonged exposure to the sun. The body needs time to adjust. In any case the seduction of the body away from a lifestyle of convenience to one to which it is more naturally suited again takes time. But the body repays you for this consideration, as you wean it off all those substitutes for healthy exercise in the open air. You know that the sun's warmth on the skin, the quiet intermittently broken by the sea birds and seals, is what the body and the mind seek — when given the choice.

I recognise the face by the road. It's Jon from Minnesota where 'there's a lot of wide open grassland, some timber — I know a place where cedarwood grows, now that's valuable.' He's hitched more than 30,000 miles all round the states since his 'other than honourable discharge' from the Marines.

Opposite page

Alvia Beach, just south of San Luis Obispo, is ruggedly beautiful, with wildlife in the form of seals and squirrels, and wilderness in the form of a crashed car that came off the 100 feet cliffs, and naturists who have thrown caution to the winds.

Christie. A girl who lives for her Arab horses. Away from the coast, California is a very rural state, sharing more with the cowboy West than its hi-tech image might imply.

'I got very high grades, so they put me on pumping gas,' he tells me. 'I've learnt to spot bullshit a mile off, that's what I've learnt in the Marines.'

He's obviously sure of being able to handle himself in any situation, that is something else he's acquired. He shows me his knife.

'I've never had to use this, but I carry it just in case. I've travelled 30,000 miles and always been looked after. Longest I went without food was a day and a half. Once spent 6 hours without water in the desert in Nevada. It was about 105,110, in the shade, except there was no shade, I was semi-conscious, dry throat, tongue, could hardly speak. A guy picked me up, took me to the hospital, they gave me some fluids, sent me on my way. He was waiting outside, took me all the way into Los Angeles.'

Jon is heading for Santa Barbara at the urging of a girl he knows there.

'She sounded keen,' he explains.

On the way we meet an all-American girl at a Mexican restaurant. She's blonde and bronzed, athletic and full of life.

'Now you should get a photograph of her,' says Jon, 'she's a typical American girl.'

Christie refuses to be photographed but engages in conversation. She's into horses.

'There's a lot of wild horses in America, sure, great herds of them on the Plains, they have to round them up and auction a lot of them off, they leave some young ones, the older ones can't fend for themselves. I have three Arabs; one's a gelding, it's worth $6,000. They sold one stallion for $600,000. Pity you didn't come last weekend, I was showing at Santa Barbara. I used to go in for three-day eventing, horses are always dangerous, I've got more mellow now. Got dragged along the side of a fence once, messed up all one side of me. Broke my jaw another time. Horse's head came up, going over a fence, I don't how I stayed on, my feet were out of the stirrups, we've got a video of it, guess I just went foward with the horse.'

'You don't mind taking risks?' I ask.

'Not really. Arabs are smart. I tied his head down so he kept it in the right position when I was training him. He started going backwards round the yard, round and round 20 times, so I left him and went inside. Would have left him all day. He stopped, started walking forwards. But when you're showing, they can be fine and then start showing off in the ring.'

I ask about the blondeness.

'Are you Scandinavian?'

'I'm Californian. Lots of people ask that. I'm half Irish, half German.'

'That explains it.'

'Got the Irish temper too.'

On the way into Santa Barbara — the start of southern California — you pass Los Alamos, you are entering an area with more think tanks than any other part of the country, and many of them have a military purpose. It is also where President Reagan has his 'Western White House' — a semi-arid ranch up in the hills. Later in the day I get another orientation on the area from Karen, whose photographer husband is studying at the nation's premier photographic school, also located in the town.

'This is fantasy land' she says, 'if you want to see typical American cities go to Chicago, Denver, Dallas.'

But then Karen is from Chicago, and has taken a 25% drop in salary to get a job here to help her husband through college. The rents are also 25% higher.

'They seem to be happy,' she says, 'but are they? It's not a place to have kids.'

'When is she going to start a family?'

'I'm 28. Next year I think,' she smiles. 'We're very basic in the mid-West. You get married, have families, settle down. Not like the people here. They're all the people who couldn't make it elsewhere.'

With a campus of the University of California based here, and the think tanks, there is a magical atmoshpere to the town. Its Spanish-style architecture is carefully preserved. There's a statue of Carlos III, who was Spanish King when California was first settled in 1792. Surrounded by mountains, it's as magical as Kathmandu, a creation of crystal-clear minds. All those think tanks... 'Geniuses with no drive,' Karen dismissively says of them, 'they want to be looked after.'

The magic in the air is very 20th century... it's nuclear. In the dance hall late at night, Dave who is also from the mid-West, joins us.

'He's 23 and has got problems,' Karen explains.

It could be the heavy knowledge he carries. There are 4 million people in the USA who are cleared for access to military secrets and there are 16 million classified documents listed among the myriad contracts given to the defence industries which are now enjoying a stupendous growth period.

The town is peaceful, slow, quiet, swept clean, flowers surround the motels and palms dot the town.

'The rich people in the hills keep it this way,' says Karen.

'The Russians definitely don't want war,' says Dave. 'They had an underground blast 18 months ago that went wrong, it scared the shit out of them... 150 miles were devasted. It was a doomsday weapon buried deep in a cave system. They never expected anything like it, they know what these bombs can do. They're scared.'

I wonder if he is referring to the persistent rumours of a large scale nuclear accident to the north of the Crimea area in Russia. There too, an area of at least 150 square miles was contaminated in an accident, but that was around 1977 or 79, this later megablast is dated to only 18 months ago, to the end of 83.

'I got the information from a friend in military intelligence,' says Dave.

For minds working on concepts of 'Star Wars' complexity, Santa Barbara could hardly be more peaceable. A contrast of perfect peace and infernal war. A man in cut-off jeans, a tee-shirt and a bespectacled face with some stubble waits behind me in the bank queue, he has the air of someone wielding enormous influence. In Santa Barbara you never know.

But Karen is wrong about one thing, the people are having a great time in the bar and in the dance hall off it. Those bronzed Californian girls are dancing with abandon.

'It's not like Minnesota, all Bible Belt there,' says Jon, 'the girls are difficult to get into bed. Here if a girl likes you , she'll invite you back and then wish you on your way the next morning.'

He didn't have a good day yesterday. The welfare office disallowed his claim since he admitted working within the last 30 days.

'Its on all the computers in California now,' he ruefully comments.

And his girlfriend is engaged to a 'fine specimen of a man'. He's planning where to go next. Back to Minnesota he calculates, the welfare is easier there. But by the time he's talking to Karen in the evening he's talking of going to college. He's already seen death at close quarters, it helps to explain the acceptance of whatever comes. Someone stuck a penknife into his stomach in a bar, the wound became infected, he was on the point of death, three times.

'I went out of my body watching the doctor and nurse working on me. The first time I was above an island with white people at one end and natives at the other. I didn't go down. The second time I went into a dark restful place. The third time into a gothic kind of church with knights of the round table there too.'

The bar we are in is like the Wild West in its boisterousness. A basketball match on the TV between LA (the Lakers) and Boston for the championship generates a huge roar of support for the Lakers. Girls smile at whoever they bump into. The waitresses are beautiful. One of the barmen is English, another — Tim — came here on holiday and stayed. A 55-year-old man, dressed like the great Caruso is standing on the bar and letting forth, with operatic gusto, some of his favourite songs. The crowd cheer the end of each heartfelt number.

'Great photographers have come here and failed to capture the beauty of Santa Barbara,' says the town tourist guide.

Joggers, skateboarders, roller skaters, cyclists ply up and down the beachside path leading towards East Beach where students at the beachside café dispense hamburgers and coke in their summer vacation, which has already begun in June. Another consideration for Jon to take into account.

Back in the dance hall, Karen is having a great time on the floor, as is her married friend.

'Being married in California doesn't mean anything.' mutters Jon.

The paper speculates that research shows Westerners love touching people, unlike Easterners. That's true. If they're not happy they don't show it, for on display is a cowboy's enthusiasm for life. The Wild West transposed to the coast and the defence technologies of the 21st century. A quantum leap, but there is little self-doubt on show. 'Let's party' says the electronic word display.

Ex-marine Jon who has spent two years travelling the country listening to demons in his head telling him that a climactic change is about to occur. He knows the land, naturally predicts that California will be hit by earthquakes, and explains the war-like feeling of the South East as being an inheritance from the warrior tribes who lived there 1,000 years ago.

Opposite page
Santa Barbara is an idyllically beautiful town of some 75,000 souls. Prices are high, because of its popularity. Here think tanks, which you suspect of thinking the unthinkable, exist in undisturbed tranquility.

On Malibu Beach you'll find Alice's Restaurant — yes, the one where you can get anything you want. There's a sense of exclusivity in the air. It's where Madonna staged her wedding shortly after the world examined her in close-up detail in *Penthouse.* The houses here of the film stars fetch millions. But the food in Alice's is good, the views along the beach are magnificent and the cost of the food is not too expensive. Yet there is an indefinable feeling that everyone is on display. Across at the next table is a young writer/composer who's won a prize from MTV, the 24-hour cable music station that's now promoting groups in an all-powerful way. The prize-winner is being taken to see all the sights and sounds of the LA music industry. Where else but Alice's Restaurant for lunch? A couple neck under the pier. Unaware that their own little meal is providing sustenance for all the diners.

'Typical Californian scene,' mutters the MTV executive who wears velvet around the collar of his suit. The winner remains studiously unexcited by the whole scene, as though it's all about to become his.

Off the public beach there are houses lining the shore for two miles and more in the direction of LA which shows up distantly on the horizon round the bay. Each house is entirely different from the rest as they stand side by side along the beach front. Even these houses are worth hundreds of thousands, no gardens, just an exclusive address — on Malibu Beach. All architect-designed, all expressing their owner's private fantasy. A futurist construction in curving lines of concrete and glass, a Swiss chalet, a Spanish dusty pink hacienda, the variations go on and on, each outvieing the other.

Walking along in the sea swell on the almost deserted white grained beach, a blonde woman appears on her verandah further up and studiedly drapes herself with legs stretched out as we come into view — a siren temptress. As we draw closer her husband/lover comes out and begins to wrap himself around her. They are playing to the gallery of two. Interruptions are few and far between here, the houses' proximity increases the distance between each fantasy lived out on the beach. Further along an Ernest Hemingway character with deeply tanned face and full beard approaches with his walking stick, his woman and three dogs, each of an exotic breed.

He strides on past, peering into the stiff breeze. (All down the coast this strong wind has been blowing from the North, early June and the temperature has yet to rise much above 60-65 along the coast, the northern winds take 10-15 degrees off the heat just the other side of the coastal mountains.)

Malibu is half a preparation for the sights and sounds, comings and goings of LA. The original Spanish settlers liked to ride their horses fast. From its settlement in 1781, Los Angeles (its name in full means Our Lady Queen of the Angels) has grown phenomenally. The unsettled plain lay between mountains and was watered by one river. The city is now supplied by water that comes from hundreds of miles away in the mountains. Within the city limits live 3,000,000 souls. In the surrounding urban areas another 5-6,000,000. The metropolis stretches for 40 miles end to end down the coast and almost as far inland. In stark contrast to the barrenness of the area, LA seethes with life and vitality.

Opposite page

Alice's Restaurant has managed to preserve some of its charm along with its fame after the 1970 film. Good food, good views along Malibu beach.

A young man is arrested by police in a suburban area of quiet white houses and carefully cultivated gardens. Three police cars, each with a man and woman team, have descended upon him after what looks like petty pilfering. Neighbours gather in the driveway as the six police officers face their captive, his hands pinioned by manacles behind his back. Each police officer carries a long baton, their captive looks young, handsome and affluent. He is still quietly defiant as an officer leads him across the road to his patrol car. The woman member of a patrol team drives up and asks what I'm photographing.
'I thought there was going to be some action,' I reply
'Just a little action,' says the male driver laconically and then drives off into the teeming city, still wide open for the successful to express any and every desire. A big open limousine shoots past on the edges of the suburb of Hollywood. A brief glimpse of a blonde at the wheel, a GB plate on the back of the limo and its gone, gone into some other fantasy of wealth and power and influence.

Sunset Strip — the long boulevard leading from Santa Monica by the sea to West Hollywood and passing under the hills rising above the plain where the rich live in immaculately tended roads lined with evergreen trees that appear just as perfect as the houses. Nothing is out of place, the gentle curve of trees leads off into a dark warm night of mystery and suspense. But then they would in Beverly Hills. Down below, the lights of LA sparkle in the desert air. It is full moon. People come and go, shouting out from the sidewalks and the passing cars. It is Saturday night. Party time. The clubs on Sunset Strip disgorge their stunningly clad clientele. The women mostly displaying a lot of leg and dressed in clinging black body stockings or white ones (Expandex — a shiny body-hugging material — has become big). Others wear glittering blue dresses, or red or orange. Everyone has to be noticed. The man on the stage — inbetween announcing the acts at the Roxy or next door at the Rainbow — invites the crowd to a party at the Museum of Rock Art on Hollywood Boulevard after the bands, New York and Brooklyn Brats, have finished playing for the evening.

A gleaming white and black chequerboard floor provides the setting for the display on the first floor of a building. There's everything from the cover of the only Blind Faith album to gold records by Fleetwood Mac. There's a poster for an obscure benefit to free John Sinclair, which announces that John Lennon and Yoko Ono will be appearing.

A girl, three weeks in town, gets into conversation,
'I'm from Galveston, Texas, 50 miles from Houston,' she introduces herself. 'Went to New York. Then thought the last place I could try was Los Angeles. It happens 24 hours a day here. One long party. There's always somewhere to go, something to do. (That appears to be true, as I reflect that all the unlimited drink at the Museum has cost just $2.50).
'We want everyone to enjoy themselves,' says the man in the long evening jacket and jeans.
That man over there owns the place,... some connection with the 'new' Chrysler company taking the exhibition on tour. A connection that dates from the time before the car companies were making 10 billion a year. Chrysler is now back in favour and seems to be sponsoring less rock art.

In a quiet LA suburb three squad cars arrive after a call and apprehend a man. Once handcuffed, he is interviewed in the back garden before being led away.

Opposite page
A club on Sunset Boulevard. The clothes are stylish and wayout. Style is in, conformity out.

Previous page
Los Angeles by night seen from the vantage point of Beverly Hills, where the homes have open windows to display the wealth inside.

Beaches, bays, yachts and tourists scattered along the coast road leading south from LA. At Laguna Beach, just outside the southern extent of the LA conurbation, I stop at The Great Australian Bite (study a map of Australia to get the pun). I ask what Australians are doing on the East Coast at the same time as I realise that it is just across the Pacific Ocean (even if that does cover 35% of the world's surface).

'Well, why not?,' the rather pale Australian behind the counter replies.

'I'm from Brisbane, over here to set up franchises for Australian meat products.'

It occurs to me that the Australian coastal highway is very similar around Queensland and Sydney. 'So it's easier doing business here?'

'Wouldn't say that. We'll just see how it works, give it a try. Where are you heading?'

'South down the coast road.'

'We get a lot of Australians heading south, when they see us they pull up nearly causing pile-ups everytime.'

(I'm half-Australian, by ancestry at least, understand the shock of the familiar for an Antipodean).

Looking at the road map I notice that there are a lot of Indian reservations halfway to San Diego, some 10 to 20 miles in from the coast, and decide to detour. Once in the mountains the people and houses of the coast quickly drop away, there are dairy farmers here and breeders of Arab horses. Eventually I find the Pala Mission Indian Reservation after coming to one dead end where the new suburban developments gave out in a valley that emanated a strange sensation. It was perfectly quiet, then a bird started calling in splendid isolation, it could have been an Indian calling out, a man masquerading as an animal so strange did it sound. Now I am among the Indians in their reservation, a man watches from his long low bungalow while I photograph it, then sends his wife out to ask what I am doing.

'What are you photographing the house for?' she asks with a smile.

'I just want a photograph of a typical Indian house,' I reassure her.

The Indians haven't lost their acuity of vision, though much has been lost.

'Are you from here?' I ask the woman, who is turning to fat like many of her people. The older ones tend to be blown up to enormous proportions.

'No another resevation.'

She goes away after shyly agreeing to be photographed.

For no particular reason I note my harsh black shadow on the baked ground ringed by semi-barren mountains. It is not prime land. Another Indian comes up who looks bright eyed and lives in a well-kept house with a newish car. I tell him I'm from London.

'You're a long way from home' he says and saunters off, at ease on his land.

My first intimation of where I had arrived was on Malibu Beach, coming off it after the long walk with the combination of wind and sun working upon me, my face was turning deep red. A Mexican with a black cowboy hat above his glowing dark face had asked if I was alright. To him, I must have looked out of place in this sun-beaten land. The sun rays, the winds, the sea spray all attack north European skin with a vengeance. My feet burn from having spent two hours out in the heat yesterday, the cold Pacific water flowing down from the

An Indian on a reservation half way to San Diego from LA. He was one of the few not bloated out by beer.

Previous page

The group New York pump out their latter-day rock to an appreciative, discerning audience in a minimally decorated, avant garde club on the strip. The girl singer of the warm-up group Brooklyn Brats, confessed she hadn't slept for days. In music you have to go to LA or New York to succeed. This was the group's first appearance on the West Coast, and they gave off signs that they were proud as hell.

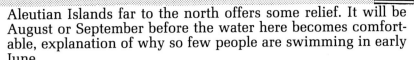

Aleutian Islands far to the north offers some relief. It will be August or September before the water here becomes comfortable, explanation of why so few people are swimming in early June.

Further into the reservation, I come to the mission itself, a Spanish church built in 1816. To reach this spot the Spanish from New Spain (Mexico) made a painful journey of 1,000 miles overland while ships eventually made rendezvous with them. The decision to develop Upper California was made to thwart Russian expansion as fur traders worked in the north. Nine missions were set up along the California coast — hence the saints' names, Santa Barbara, Santa Cruz, San Francisco...

The Indians in California do not have a history of warfare, they helped the missionaries, who were in any case accompanied by soldiers. It helps to explain why some 170 years later there are a lot of Mexican visitors to a 'fair' where Indian jewellery and crafts are sold. A group of Mexicans in cowboy hats are singing in the mission's earthern square. Gradually I learn to make out the Indians from the Mexicans. The Indians are usually blown out from beer, indeed all the Indian men are clutching beer cans. But then any creature in captivity or a confined space needs a sense of purpose, needs to be able to control its environment. Unproductive land and government welfare checks have undermined the Indians' morale and self-worth. They aimlessly wander in an alcoholic haze, happy to deal with the Mexicans, less so with the more recently arrived north Europeans. California only really started to develop after the end of the Second World War. Millions of soldiers, sailors and airmen were stationed here as were many wartime factories, a lot of people stayed on after it was over.

New housing developments, advertising superb views, push into the interior. The Indians have to adjust again. At the next reservation there is Renich Indian Bingo. Californians' cars are incongrously stacked outside a large modern bingo hall.

On reaching San Diego I meet Kerry and her friend — in town to be briefed by a hair shampoo manufacturer on why their products are so good. Kerry has got the religion and tells me why she will make a fortune as a demonstrator to hairdressers of all the product's myriad advantages.

'I started cutting hair at 14,' she enthuses, 'made great bald patches in my sister's hair. Been cutting hair ever since.'

Kerry and her friend are from Yuma, a 3-hour drive away just over the border in Arizona. They're on the Colorado River and a dam has created a lush fertile land out of semi-desert. The two women are warm and friendly.

So is the weather in San Diego.

'We've got a swimming pool and temperatures up in the 90s, but it's nothing like this,' Kerry's sunburnt friend mutters painfully. 'It must be the sea.'

All roads lead to California in the West.

'I've been up to San Francisco where they're all homosexual and doing drugs. But that's not typical America. In Utah, they don't take coffee, smoke or drink but they all have four, five, 20 children. But that's not typical America. In Arizona, they're friendly, sunny people. Different again. Best thing I ever did when I left the mines in Lancashire 20 years ago,' says my motel owner host.

He's laid back and drawling like San Diego people. Sunset is a brilliant palm-tree-studded spectacular. Here on the borders of Mexico you feel you can unwind. Though Kerry did say one thing worth keeping in mind.

'To write about something, you have to live it, right?'

'Yes.'

'America can be a dangerous place, do you know that?'

'The thought had occurred to me.'

# THE MUSIC MACHINE

MTV arrives again. In the person of John Kennedy, a cameraman working on a $1 million video for a group out of New York who are, as yet, unknown. He predicts MTV will make $10 million from the video. Shooting began in San Francisco.

'I got a beautiful shot of a red moon reflected off the sea... the full moon too.'

The video progresses from the civilisation of San Francisco to the 'jungle' of San Diego zoo. Shooting begins at 10 the next morning. John is downing a few drinks in a beach bar, before the work day begins tomorrow, he's just flown in from San Francisco. Over the drinks I hear some of his life. Kennedy. Yes, he's Irish-American. On one side the Kennedys, on the other the Walshes.

'All my nephews and nieces are half-Yugoslav, half-Hungarian, me I'm 100% Irish-American, my family came over in the 1870s.'

Mention of Vietnam. I tell him about the news media claiming 100,000 vets have committed suicide since they returned.

'Is that right? 53,000 were killed, I know. I volunteered for the Navy Reserve, figured if I was sent there, at least I'd be off the coast on a ship. Never got out there. Discharged in 68. I became a sort of hippy after that. Guess you could say I'm a liberal, I'd vote for Socialism in America. But I'm doing OK. Paid for my house, pay $560 a month on the mortgage. I'm out of New York but I live in Austin, Texas. My girlfriend's there. She gets pissed off at all the travelling I do. Couple of months ago I was 1,000 miles south in Mexico, it's tropical there. Austin's nice. A river. Lots of music. We're having a jazz festival in July. There's a great jazz festival in New Orleans in May, you've been there? Jim Morrison, the American poet. He's a lot more appreciated now he's dead. Grace Slick? She's still around, had an alcohol problem for a bit, she's still with Jefferson Starship.'

Beside us at the bar is a dark-haired girl who asks me to shift my seat along a couple of feet. She's got probing black eyes to match the dark hair. I ask where's she from.

'San Diego.'

'But are your parents American?'

'I'm a quarter Cherokee, see, the high cheekbones, the slanting eyes. I'm vegetarian, have been for years. Weigh 108. I used to run for 20 miles a day. Have you tried ginseng? It's great for the body. I do aerobics, used to be into frisbees, won a few championships. I do some modelling, animal skins are my favourite.'

Trixie is slim, petite, 5'4". Her only apparent vice seems to be drink which she consumes at the bar as the sun goes down casting a blue spectral light on the surfers who have suddenly appeared as black dots in the intense blueness of the ocean.

I hear some more of her life. She's 21. Rooms with a much older man.

'It's purely platonic. He does a lot of coke, makes him look younger but he's crazy. He gets high then goes out and drives his car, slams it into other cars.'

And her boyfriend?

'Oh I guess I'm in love. Had a big row last Saturday night (it's Monday) He fired a Magnum .22 at me.'

'With live bullets?'

'Yeah I walked out on him.'

'How far did the bullets miss by?'

Opposite page

Trixie used to jog 20 miles a day, as well as work out in a gym, as well as winning a few frisbee championships. You have to fit in southern California. Are health clubs the new singles bars? Or is it just hype for the latest John Travolta film? Who wants Olivia Newton John anyway? To be continued...

Previous page

'It never rains in California.' From Santa Barbara to the border it's sunny most the year. San Francisco can get chilly and misty though, no guaranteed tan there.

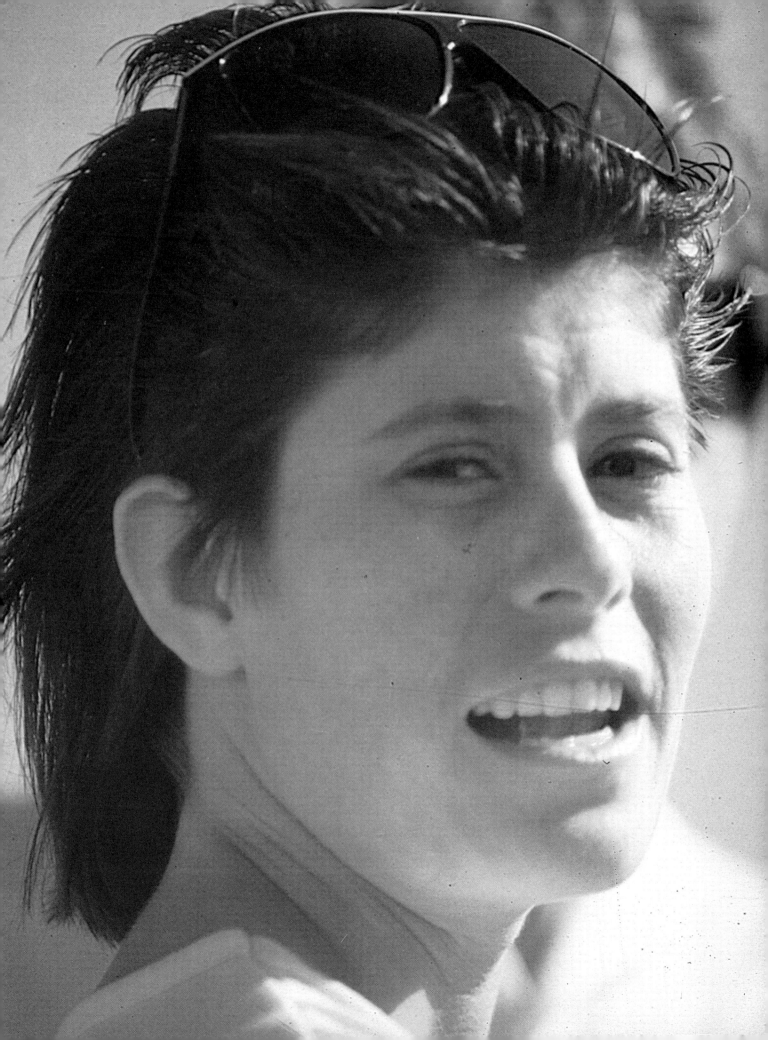

'A couple of inches. I had an abortion a month ago. There's no way I want a baby at the moment, you know. My boyfriend's got a problem with his parents, especially his mother. He's 28 and all mixed up. I've known him 4 years. I don't really enjoy sex. I've only had 7 orgasms in that time, you know.'
'You think you'll go back?'
'Well I kind of love him, but if he's gonna shoot at me, that's it.' Her boyfriend sounds the very jealous type. And her room-mate.
'I daren't tell him about this.'
Remembering the bullet shots I agree.
'You know guys stroke themselves reading Playboy, that's how a lot of them get their kicks. Sure I get Playgirl, but it's just to look at their bodies, not to masturbate by.'

California life is a succession of incidents. By the sea, the ever present wind blows away most of caution. But that's no excuse for running the stop signs, which Trixie urges.

'I have to work tomorrow, modelling. You should see San Diego zoo.' (The zoo again, it must be good).

On the bridge linking San Diego and Coronado, there are signs prominently displayed at its approach and in the middle of its full 250 feet elevation saying 'We care about you, call this number for suicide counselling.' Life is tough for the young. An article in the paper says that in the local high school, two thirds of the way through the academic year, 18 students have attempted, or threatened to attempt, suicide.

I remember hitchhiker Jon's comment.
'The people have a very fragile lifestyle, they have all these props keeping them up, they get to 30 and lose them, say my life's not worth living.'

Those lost Indian tribes.. 'You should feel at home here, much more than the other people, you've been here a long time.'

The quarter Cherokee girl understands that the interruptions of the traffic signs are inconsequent in the dark, moonlit, ocean-surrounded landscape. The pound of the surf fades away on the beach, the tiny houses pile up one upon the other — it is here you disappear into a lifestyle removed from the great sweep of the land, where problems become magnified and where for want of someone to talk to, the final urge takes over. Strange when so much life beats within the land, where beauty is the final determinant of success. Joggers pass by the window late at night, in tune with the surge... of the ocean... of life.

Previous page
Pacific Beach at San Diego, early in the morning. The men have slept rough and now stir for the day, just a little unsteady on their feet, but the ocean is beautiful and blue.

Opposite page
It's still considered daring to go topless on the average American beach. This rare sight was spotted on Pacific Beach. European nonchalence about nudity has yet to reach America.

Another of San Diego's beaches is at Coronado across the spectacular harbour bridge. Called Silver Strand Beach, who knows what you might see there?

Heading for the beach, the car radio playing a blast from the past, 'Everyone's gone surfin', surfin' USA'. It's a beautiful day with the weatherman calling for 82, the surf's five feet high at 'the American city with the best surfing beaches in the nation' according to the San Diego DJ. I discover that they have left out the thick mist in their description of the beaches — at least the one where all the dedicated surfers go, Black's Beach. Owned by the University of California it used to be most famous as one of America's few topless beaches. But that was another era, America is more conservative now, still grappling with a frontier conservatism as far as women are concerned, no wonder they rebel. An armed guard at the Salk Institute watches me carefully as I inspect the cliffs. It's a treacherous route down to the beach far below and I return to the made-up road that — although barred to cars — leads circuitously and steeply to the shore under great cliffs. (It leads off from La Jolla Farm Road where it meets Blandford Road). There are only surfers on the beach, dotted about like sea birds on the advancing high rollers. The mist prevents any attempt at beach lolling. It is a very similar scene to what would be happening in Australia on the other side of the ocean. The surfers look similarly dedicated and awesomely fit. They give off the feeling of being in touch with the world and stand out because of it.

The next beach in towards the town in San Diego is La Jolla Cove, a suburban beach for families and younger surfers. A large population on the sand, where the mist has cleared, watches the few people actually in the water even though it's reached 63 degrees this far south. As always, an initial reluctance to enter the sea is compensated by the feeling of freedom it gives once in those rising and falling waves. The surf is strong, it beats you back, drives you, turns you upside down in the lash of the breaking waves — as I discovered the day before on the more isolated Silver Strand Beach, reached off Highway 75 once you have crossed the spectacular bridge linking San Diego and Coronado. At the two-mile long Silver Strand you can catch sight of porpoise, dolphins and — in January — whales as they head south to their breeding grounds. It's here that you can feel the full blast of the mighty Pacific, not always as calm as its name would suggest.

However, you don't go to a town to find isolated beaches. San Diego is a holiday town and naval base with nearly 1 million inhabitants. It is surprising that one of its main beaches, Pacific Beach, can be so relatively undeveloped and unspoilt — apart from the great strands of seaweed that come ashore each day (and are efficiently cleared by beach tractors early each morning). It's a long stretch of white sand with some sheltering cliffs at its northern end, where in relative seclusion you can spend a rewarding day getting into beach life. Either from the sands or from one of the bars and cafés which lie behind the promenade. This narrow promenade is a constant parade of joggers and cyclists and characters — some of the rougher ones obviously sleep out. More people disgorge from battered vans or use the relatively cheap apartments that line the shore. I check into the Pacific Sands Motel, right on the beach so that you can hear the distant roar of the breakers at night. It's run by Pete, the miner mentioned earlier. His Japanese wife died 4 years ago, Peter has compassion and an interest in those he meets.

Previous page

'Look at the light on the water,' said the man at Alvia Beach as he passed. He was right. America can be very beautiful, once allowed to be.

La Lahina Beach House. A great bar. A great stereo system. A great clientelle. On Pacific Beach. Watch the sun go down in all those warm Californian colours.

'Benders' for breakfast by the sea. Afternoons on the terrace at La Lahina Beach House. Almost a club, where the 20 and 30 year-olds steadily drink the pitchers of beer, laugh away the afternoon fanned by the sea breeze and listen to sounds of XHITZ — 'only the T is silent, if you don't play us loud something doesn't sound quite right.'

The newspapers filter through the odd and interesting news as a day passes lazily enough overlooking the ocean surrounded by banter. The New York Stock Exchange reaches a new high. Time Magazine predicts the economy is waking up from a slump. Orange County (part of the LA urban area) takes the prize for the greatest number of white collar crimes under investigation in the nation. Leaving Fort Lauderdale/Miami and New York behind.

'It's the boom in land values and the sunshine that does it,' explains a local commentator. 'These people have done so well out of their property investments that they really do believe commodity trading companies can return them 10% interest a month, even though the government only pays 8% a year.'

President Reagan's tax reform plans highlight the revealing news that half of America's top 250 companies pay no tax, while there are at least 9,000 millionaires who also pay no tax. People anxious to find tax shelters provide easy money for the unscrupulous. Then there is the notorious Bank of America 'scam' under investigation, which has resulted in the Bank losing $96 million and when fully unravelled the bank and others may have collectively lost $500 million. Certainly the Bank of America's first quarter profits have been wiped out.

There's another news item that catches the eye. A man who has died from AIDS in an LA prison hospital. He was jailed for sex with an underage girl. The counsellors to the girl disagree about whether she should be told.

'We don't understand fully how AIDS gets transmitted. It can, we believe, be transmitted by blood or semen. Anal sex often results in bleeding. 80% of those exposed to the virus don't go down with the disease's manifestations. Stress, lifestyle, exposure to previous venereal disease affect the body's defences.'

Middle America becomes a little more aware of the rampantly promiscuous and often anonymous sex indulged in by the homosexual population. The gay plague they call it. I think about the wan face of the man with his friend in a bar on Fisherman's Wharf, San Francisco . He looks thin and weak. Weight loss and lethargy are two of the signs of the killer disease in action. His 'friend' asks him if he takes sugar in his coffee — the victim in his turn seeks out further victims.

Having found the sun and warmth in San Diego, I head back up the coast towards San Francisco, giving myself the opportunity to re-evaluate some of the places on the way. Everything looks different with the sun out.

In Los Angeles the temperature in Hollywood is 85, while on the beaches it is in the high 70s. The first smog warning of the year is posted above the highway. The TV broadcasts that the smog is hazardous to everyone's health. On the beaches that line the fringe of LA — perfect golden beaches — there's no sign of the haze. At Manhattan Beach there's acres of space, houses leading right down to the beach and friendly little restaurants. The attractions of LA living are here to see. Along up the coast towards Malibu the beaches become more crowded. I pass the John Paul Getty museum on Pacific Highway with a reputed $20 million that must be spent on art each year, if it is to preserve its charitable status.

Open air living is an art in itself. I find myself drawn back past Malibu, past Santa Barbara, to Alvia Beach. The sun is going down behind the isolated cove. A few campers are on the beach. There is a perfect quiet and remoteness with grand views from the headland across the bay. A party of 8 teenage girls take up their viewpoint on the rocks of the headland as the colours take on a deeper hue. On the beach there were some squirrels scurrying up the cliff face, the showers of dislodged stones advertising their presence. The basking seals have gone. There is only the sound of the sea, the glowing gold colour in the sunset-lit water and a distant transistor playing. It's easy to feel at peace with the world now, removed from the hustle and bustle of mainstream America.

But it's to that world that you must eventually return. A large number of economists predict that 1986 will see the beginning of a slump. Japanese goods are extolled and sold or attacked by American manufacturers. Reagan continues his 'fireproof' act, undisturbed by links revealed to President Nixon in both his 1984 campaign and his present foreign policy. Did his advisers know about the colon tumour before the election? The Senate approves $38 million of 'humanitarian' aid for the Nicaraguan 'contras'. Two helicopters are shot down on the country's border. The bush fire begins to burn.

Down in San Diego, where you can see the illegal immigrants from over the border working as gardeners in the homes of the rich near Black's Beach, you start to sense the reality of life just a little further south. A teacher takes a party of schoolchildren along the beachfront in San Diego. 'That's north, and that's south,' she says, indicating which way is which. Almost all the children are Mexican. They are too young to realise from where they have so recently come.

Further inland and further up the coast, I pass a cowgirl astride a palomino horse. I'm now in the hot inner valley of Monterey Peninsula, I stop and take a picture of the cowgirl. 'Cut it out man, cut it out,' she says, her black eyes focusing on the camera, 'I'm just having problems.'

The horse canters awkwardly past, waving its head from side to side.

She's wearing a cowboy hat, tee shirt and big leather boots but her black hair, deeply tanned face and dark eyes stamp her as unmistakably Mexican in origin. The accent is pure Californian however.

'You're a true American cowgirl,' I tell her.

'I wish that were true,' she smiles, finally relaxing, convinced I only wanted to photograph her because she couldn't get the big handsome horse completely under control. She gallops off at full tilt, splendid in the baking heat. An American dream.

I remember John Kennedy explaining the mixture of the races.

'The different countries didn't start mixing till the 20s and 30s.' But then he was from New York. A researcher discovers that Elvis Presley has a great great great Cherokee Indian grandmother. And that he fell apart after 1958 when his mother Gladys died. Some Americans have been here a long time. But the energy now is concentrated in the south of the country, in the sunbelt. California's wealth is founded on its agriculture, oil, gold and copper, its defence industries and their hi-tech spin-offs, its entertainment conglomerates. You sense that beneath the swirl of people arriving from every state in the nation, the Californians do have a genius for communication, a compulsive need to strike up a conversation, an eye for the opportunity.

'The two aims in California are to be rich and beautiful,' Jon from Minnesota explained. 'The people who are rich and ugly are very bad indeed. And the beautiful ones quickly become rich.'

But another image clouds the mind. The 1940 World Fair. The children are wearing all their finery, they look perplexed at the lack of festivity in the air, the adults look on abstractly, knowing that the world is about to change utterly and that dreams will have to be deferred...

San Francisco looks good in the golden evening sunset. It has become a centre for the arts. Not bad for the lawless town of the '49 gold rush when vigilantes had to roam the streets to provide any semblance of protection. You wonder if prizes so quickly won will just as quickly be let go.

'The Americans are such piglets,' remarked that Arab-riding country girl.

The most dangerous thing she had attemped was paragliding.

'Its pretty scary looking down from higher than a 10 storey building. I don't know how they got me up. I had some drinks first.'

Now she's feeding her sheep and horses after waitressing all day. The farmers are finding it hard to pay their way, something's out of kilter in the economy. In a country that's still young, brave and agriculturally rich, the worrying stock analysts on Wall Street seem a far-off spectre unconnected with the land that the 'long time' Americans know and feel at home in. They preferred to invest in South America...perhaps to their cost.

The 8-mile bridge from Oakland to San Francisco seen at dawn. Good morning America, how are ya?

**Niagara Falls.** If you feel brave you can take a boat that approaches very close to the thunderous spray at the Falls' bottom.

**New England.** See the leaves in Fall.

**New York.** Take a bus ride into Harlem — you'll be the only white person there. Do it in daylight and take the bus out, it gets dangerous on the fringes where you meet the poor whites.

**Pennsylvania.** Stop off on a side road and wash your face in one of the numerous crystal clear rivers and streams. You'll feel thoroughly refreshed and changed.

**North Carolina.** The Cape Hatteras national seashore is a long string of land out in the sea. Absolutely spectacular. Don't forget Surf City further south.

**New Jersey.** Ocean Beach is everything a young sea resort should be. And for something completely different there's the long boardwalk at Atlantic City.

**Washington DC.** The Library of Congress runs numerous participatory events. The Smithsonian has an outstanding reputation among museums, while the Kennedy Center for the Performing Arts is lavish and potentially rewarding.

**Virginia.** At Natural Bridge on I 80 you can find an idyllic spot with one of the oldest trees in the East (it looks very dead). There's also Skyline Drive a little further north on I 80 where you can turn off for a splendid drive to Washington.

**Georgia.** The Suwannee drifts lazily along at the border with Florida. Hire a boat and meander with it.

**Florida.** Home of the John F Kennedy Space Center. And of Alligator Alley where the long cross-country road in the south is likely to have unexpected hazards in the shape of the occasional marauding croc.

**Hawaii.** You're really on a tropical island in the mighty Pacific. The problems of the world fade into their true perspective surrounded by so much ocean.

**Alaska.** The Government actually gives you a tax credit for living here. So if you want to confront your true self in the wilderness...

**Appalachian Mountains.** Heading south, off the highways, you'll meet a sleepy old America.

**The Grand Canyon.** Everyone's overcome by it.

**Alabama.** There's oil money to be earned in the coastal areas.

**Mississippi.** You could ride the river to the sea. It's continental-sized and has a lot to tell you about the country if you're open to its murmur.

**New Orleans.** One of the few racial melting pots in America. Unique.

**Texas.** The big one. You'll feel taller. Take in a dance and watch the girls move. The south of the state is a place to find the warmth in winter.

**New Mexico.** Just drive through the wide open spaces and sense the civilisations who have passed this way before you.

**Colorado.** The new America in the making, skiing, beautiful views, a progressive university, you'll like it.

**Arizona.** Yuma is a green paradise created out of the desert.

**California.** What happens when the frontier spirit meets the ocean. Genuinely friendly.

**Los Angeles.** You'll get a buzz out of whatever you do.

**San Francisco.** One of everyone's favourite American cities. Yes, do take a cable car ride.

**The Rockies.** Cowboy country all along their length

**Nebraska.** Now you're in real farming country. And the heart of the defence system with the Strategic Air Command stationed in Omaha.

**Tennessee.** Still has a flavour of the 18th century pioneers in its old fashioned civility.

**Money Saving Tips**
* There is no such thing as a fixed price in hotels, especially if you are prepared to take your custom elsewhere when the ploy doesn't work. Ask for the special rate.
* Many plush business hotels charge special weekend rates in the big cities
* If you plan to visit a lot of places there's air tickets available with only a time limit on them
* Airline stand-bys are a lot cheaper but check out all the requirements and be prepared for the odd disappointment
* Car hire companies let you drive cars for virtually nothing if you will deliver them to a location. Easier in mid-America than on the coasts.
* Most car companies give discounts to a host of different organisations and companies, ask for a discount
* Change foreign money in banks not hotels, a lot of hotels won't change it for you outside the big cities
* It's cheaper to stay on the outskirts of big cities by a long way
* If you can sing for your supper there's a good chance your offer will be taken up in a town
* Take out fully comprehensive medical and car insurance
* If you plan your journey ahead, ring round and compare the deals

**Travel tips**
* It's very tiring travelling at night, try to do most of it in the day
* The Interstate highways are well provided with motels, the back roads less so
* Waitresses are wonderful sources of information
* Carry your money in two separate places, make a note of emergency numbers for refunds on traveller checks
* Not everyone accepts credit cards, you need a little cash, but traveller checks are very easy to change
* If you go over your credit limit on a credit card try ringing the HQ and explaining.
* Many of the more expensive shops and hotels are on line to the credit card centers, don't rely on your bills taking weeks to catch up with you

**Avoiding trouble**
* Be careful who you get talking to
* Politeness and friendliness bring about the same reaction as a rule
* Don't provide temptation by advertising your wealth in the wrong places
* Drug addicts can't be reasoned with, if confronted do not inflame the situation unless you can give superb account of yourself
* Appreciate people on their own terms... that way you won't be a threat to them
* Help arrives in the most unexpected forms, travel hopefully and arrive safely

following page

Girl with hat. A day comes to its end. On the headland above Alvia Beach a party of teenage girls gather to watch the sunset. Peace perfect peace. And hope for the future.

The old church in st Augustine, Florida. Over 70% of Americans attend church during the course of a month.

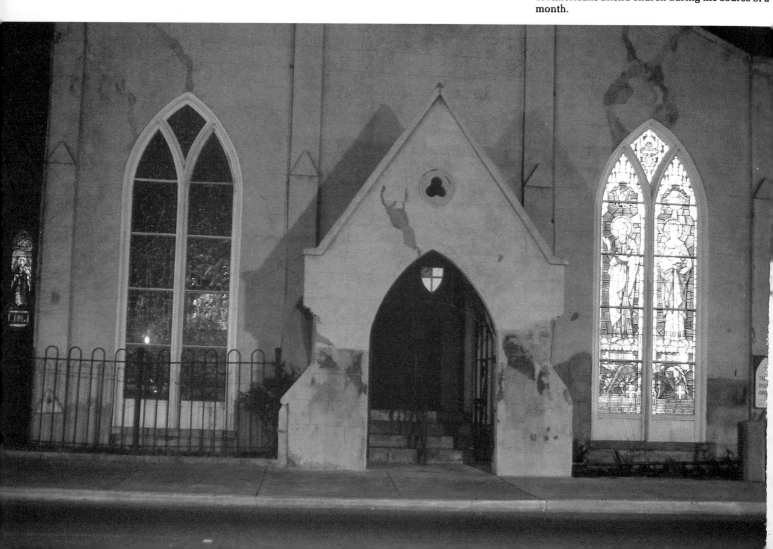